CH00970969

ROY FULLER

HOME AND DRY

HOME AND DRY

Memoirs III

ROY FULLER

Where's Commander All-a-Tanto?
Where's Orlop Bob singing up from below?
Where's Rhyming Ned? Has he spun his last canto?
Where's Jewsharp Jim? Where's Rigadoon Joe?
                                            — Herman Melville

London Magazine Editions

1984

London Magazine Editions also publish the following by Roy Fuller:

Autobiography
Souvenirs
Vamp Till Ready

Poetry
The Reign of Sparrows

The publishers acknowledge the financial assistance of the Arts Council

Published by London Magazine Editions
30 Thurloe Place, London SW7
© Roy Fuller
SBN 904388 476

Printed by Unwin Brothers Limited,
The Gresham Press,
Old Woking, Surrey

Contents

1.   Aflatun and Aristu

When I heard I was going abroad, love,
I thought I was going to die;
We walked arm in arm to the road, love,
We looked arm in arm to the sky.

- W. M. Praed

When I set off for Ceylon in April 1942 I started a journal, an
indication of my sense of the momentous, for I am no diarist, being
indolent, and bothered even by the elementary problems of the
genre, such as which tense to employ. I kept the thing with moderate
conscientiousness for a couple of months, and shall use the material
here, having just re-read it, surprised at its moments of interest. I
thought I had ransacked it of anything valuable for my novel *The
Perfect Fool* (1963), but I see now there may be point in presenting
the comparatively brief narrative at greater length.

Questions arise of what memory can add to such a record, and
of the rival 'truths' of actuality and hindsight. Some things unnoted
have stayed vividly in mind. On the other hand, I had forgotten the
apparent vehemence of my disillusion with men and ideas. Taking
one thing with another, I do not doubt being able truthfully to
present this journal with the added perspective of forty years. I say
'truthfully' but really the word should be 'honestly', for neither
pure memory nor memory plus documentation can bring back the
'truth'. As to this, and the defects of memory, see the fine passages
about her early life in *The Swan in the Evening* by Rosamond
Lehmann.

The journal was written in the first few pages of a Stationery

Office notebook issued to me at Robert Gordon's College, Aberdeen, on a Royal Navy course preparatory to training as a radar mechanic. Sheets of more official guff seem to have been torn out before the journal was started. On the cover I had put my name, number and rating, and the Aberdeen address, but on going thence to Lee-on-the-Solent and being re-rated, I had crossed out the address and substituted 'L/A.F.(D.F.)' for 'Ord/Sea'. The 'L/' must have been added when promotion to Leading Hand came at the end of the Lee course. 'A.F.(D.F.)' meant 'Air Fitter (Direction Finding)', radar ('radiolocation', the English term still in general use) being considered so secret as not to be bruited in the classification of personnel.

As recounted in the second volume of these memoirs, *Vamp Till Ready*, I had left my wife and infant son in genteel digs near Seafield Park, the Royal Naval Air Station overflow establishment not far from Lee. Our last meeting (or, more properly, parting) had been that described (with a pathos I have never been entirely happy about) in my poem 'Goodbye For a Long Time', but a sort of final farewell, silent, more Keatonish than Chaplinesque, was made at a distance in the drive of Seafield Park; Kate on a borrowed bicycle, myself peering out with others over the tailboard of a R.N. truck. From Lee the Ceylon draft was trucked to R.N.B., Portsmouth and entrained at the railway station there. Then ensued an all-night journey to Liverpool, in sharp contrast to the family life recently tasted, a depth of proletarian service existence scarcely plumbed before, not even in Chatham Barracks, where at least frequent escape 'ashore' could be envisaged.

I tried to read *The White Cockatoo*, an indifferent whodunnit by Mignon G. Eberhart (I hope I ascribe it rightly, though no fictive talent could have offset the night's debits). But mostly I dozed, or overlooked a game of baccarat at the nearest table in the compartment, played for what seemed notably high stakes by four Air Mechanics. One, red-haired, pimpled, often used an appellation (then a novelty to me) imputing bastardy and a certain homosexual practice, and reasonably enough queried, as a matter of propriety, by the printers' proof-reader of the day when I employed it in *The Perfect Fool*. Another of the Air Mechs, for some reason never apparent, was nicknamed Toscanini – usually called Tosca or Toscafuckinini. The amazing extent of the *maestro's* fame thereby revealed did not strike me at the time. Tosca was rather dour, sad at losing. The stooge, as I saw him, of the four was a small, simpler man addressed as Ivan (possibly his real name) or, following a popular song of the day, Ivanskavinski Skavar (authentic spelling not guaranteed). Though derided by the others, he persisted in wagering what were regarded as miserable threepences, though, to put that stake in context, I had played family bridge not many years before for a half-penny a hundred. Simple stooge or not, Ivan subsequently hopped the troopship before it sailed, after spreading the erroneous information that he was in the sick bay. His absence was not discovered until we had been three days at sea.

The night somehow passed. The high (or low) spot of the ensuing day was disentraining at Aintree station, which could not have been a particularly jolly place even on Grand National Day. There was a bare platform, a footbridge farther up the line. As the Fleet Air Arm draft of 125 men, with bags and ammicks, and an Ordnance Corps draft, with bags and rifles, waited for transport, a few civilians watched from high on the footbridge. An essentially sentimental feeling gripped one, nurtured by the literature and photographs, even memories, of the 1914–18 war, of a doom shared with these fellow servicemen, now separated for ever from ordinary English life.

The Army eventually supplied the transport that took us to a transit camp not far away. Dust blew off the dried mud of the parade ground. As the F.A.A. ate a poor meal in the mess hall, there was the rhythmic sound of approaching boots. Words of command rang out. Some detachment of swaddies burst into the mess and barged about for advantageous places in the food queue. We were astounded, less perhaps at the uncouthness than that men should be marched to their eating place. The experience was a foretaste of what was in store on the troopship, an existence also organised by the Army. The journey and the milieu had induced boredom and pessimism, everyone deeply chokka, hoping, like the terminally ill, that some phenomenon would prevent the looming voyage or at least passage to so remote a destination – 'I never did the Japs any harm' a remark heard more than once. My Scottish friend, Willie Robertson, had a catchphrase for the disastrous strokes that fell: 'It's no' fair, it's no' right – it's a nigger's left ball.'

I wonder whether in my case woes were not slightly augmented by some nautical lore recalled from the days when my mother, in search of health, used to shuttle with the Parslews to the Isle of Man. Their home port was Fleetwood, the crossing from there said to be easier than that from Liverpool, where a battle across the prevailing current caused vessels to roll even on calm days. It would be like me to have the Irish Sea in mind when the Atlantic was in prospect. Rumour had it, however, that we were to sail in the *Capetown Castle*, a luxury passenger ship of some 22,000 tons, presumably a more stable proposition than the near ferry-boats that plied between Fleetwood and Douglas. Rumours ('buzzes'), if not actually controlling service life (for their chance of embodying future actuality was modest), lay influentially behind it, particularly at critical periods such as this; so much so that one fancifully thought of the many-tongued personification as a character in a drama of otherwise squalid naturalism – something by Ben Jonson, say, where an ironic or supernatural apparatus introduces and interrupts the strivings and disasters of the human gulls and cheats.

Rumour soon proved her power. The next day we moved to Liverpool docks, filed aboard the *Capetown Castle*, a steward at the foot of the gangway giving each man a card. This proved to indicate the number of the bunk allotted, in our case in an immense ballroom, panelled in similar style to the boardroom of my late employers, the Woolwich Equitable Building Society. The interior had been filled with bunks on the open wine-rack principle. By what I saw at once as an amazing stroke of luck, the number on my card took me to the top bunk of one of a pair, merely two bunks tall, that faced swing-doors leading from the deck, the limitations in height and breadth occasioned by the architectural features of the entrance, some slight projection of which afforded a place for a few books and other small items of kit. In the ballroom's interior were crowded alleyways, mass recumbent propinquity. 4,000 were said to be aboard: from the start queues formed for washing, eating, defecating, canteen – the last merely an aperture through which tea, biscuits, fags and nutty could be bought from rapacious merchant navy personnel.

We had embarked on 14 April, at night were pulled into the stream, and set sail at noon the following day. Initially, there were six ships in a very slow convoy; the sea at first dead calm, turning to a modest swell the next day, perhaps as the dread current came into play. The *Capetown Castle* was armed, and I was given the job of look-out on the Oerlikon gun on the port side of the bridge. This automatic weapon, oiled, black and slender, not huge, Swiss-made, novel to me, was housed in an iron-framed and concrete-bodied pill-box, reached from the deck by a vertical ladder. In time, some perfunctory account of its workings were given by the naval

4

gunners on the spot, but whether one was ever expected, in some emergency, to fire it was doubtful. The Marine C.S.M. started off by muddling the roster, so members of the gun-post crew were uncertain whether they were on watch or off. I did most of the first day, and 9 – 11.30 of the first night.

This, and the cold as we moved north into the Atlantic, set me against look-out duties (which settled down into the averagely arduous four hours on, eight off), but in retrospect having something to do in comparative isolation, if only to daydream and chat, was another stroke of luck. I am puzzled now as to the point of looking-out during the night watches, but presumably there was a chance of detecting a periscope. I remember being sceptical even vis-à-vis daylight hours, but was reassured by one with experience that it was not unknown for the thing to be spotted by an innocent and unbinoculared eye.

Soon we were sailing into the sunset, the convoy now about twenty ships, escorted by two cruisers and some destroyers. The light sky, blackish-grey sea, white rolls of foam blowing back from the noses of the westward-bound formation – such seemed newsreel clichés, not of interest compared with the miseries of going on watch, sleeping in one's clothes, the rationing of washes to two a day (for those who queued assiduously). Vanished my Wordsworthian interest in natural objects, Spenderian love of fellow men: I squirmed to recall the bullshit I had written about naval life, luckily in letters rather than verse. The even blankness of depression by no means excluded suicidal impulses, as in prisons and concentration camps.

When the swell increased many became ill, increasing the interior miasma. I myself went on eating normally but slept more, talked less, most matters of the mind subordinated to those of the body. I was full of the anxious languor and stuffiness always to some degree lurking at sea, even in 'Uncle' Fred Thompson's yacht in the Ribble estuary, to mention one of my previous principal maritime experiences.

We had with us only our personal kit (contents of a sailor's attaché case); kitbags and suitcases still in a hold, though daily promised. Till they came up, all I had left to read was *The Ring and the Book* – Everyman edition, still possessed, with my deck- and bunk-numbers written neatly in ink below my name. Underestimating tactical reading requirements was an error I repeated throughout the war, though the error was compounded by shortage.

The suicidal moods, and sickliness-without-being-sick, passed after a few days. Even at my worst I noted the excellence, even heartening quality, of Browning's poem, which seemed to me then to make Tennyson 'look horribly provincial'. But for quite a time wind, rain and endless processions of people – all through the facing swing doors – made my bunk virtually uninhabitable during the day, when it was desirable for a certain amount of lost sleep to be recovered. A greater degree of quiet could be had sitting on the broad staircase leading from the ballroom to a sun-deck. Others discovered this, too, and after a few days a notice was affixed to a bannister: OFFICERS ONLY. MARINES NOT ALLOWED ON THESE STAIRS. Despite some wag soon deleting 'ONLY. MARINES', and a semantic argument about the restrictive connotation of 'marines', the refuge was pretty effectively denied. My nerves could not be said to be in good order; and lack of sleep and exercise, and too much tea, and chocolate and biscuit eating, brought dyspepsia.

The journal for 26 April records what I think was not mild paranoia; though I shall have a further instance to recount, and in the light of *The Ordeal of Gilbert Pinfold* one sees that sea voyages are good breeding grounds for the disorder. I complained, without giving examples, that I seemed 'to be *distrusted* not to say disliked, by some, the rougher of us. I sense this. Because I am educated? A leading hand? The thing to do is to be precisely myself, not try to adapt myself to these proletarians or artisans. Very difficult – I always try to adapt myself with everyone. "Negative personality"! And perhaps (when I think about it) I am too amiable – in contrast to the times when I withdraw into my shell of books and abstraction, fearing contact. If I weren't a poet I should be a leader and (most disturbingly) vice versa!'

I reproduce this bit of psychologizing, though not typical of the journal, because the very feebleness of its expression denotes the reality of the hostility; also, it is an early specimen of my self-diagnosis of split personality, a notion I continued to express, even act out, though when echoed by reviewers and others one sees it as far too simplistic. Yes (and I use the journal's language), I loathed the smell of the 4,000 men on the *Capetown Castle*, the way they opened their uncouth mouths – more stupid than animals. I loathed the way they carelessly jostled me. Yet, as will soon be seen, longing for fraternity, admiration for revolt, were still easily roused.

The weather improved. A daily lime-juice ration appeared, and the first flying-fish. At dusk the latter resembled dragonflies; in the morning sun, swallows. The open deck became as crowded as the 'flats' had been. The continuous impromptu concert that went on *en plein air* is briefly but not badly evoked in *The Perfect Fool*. It is there characterised as mostly obscene, but I wonder if it was any more so than the entertainments now offered in clubs and pubs, and even on TV. I avoided the Sunday morning church service for naval ratings not by advancing my officially-recorded atheism but by retreating to the gun-post, which in fact overlooked the padre on the foredeck, his breeze-blown vestments surmounted by a khaki topee.

The rig of the day had become khaki shorts and shirts, issued at Lee-on-the-Solent before we left. The shorts were of curious specification, probably dating from the Kipling era. The legs were very wide and reached down to the knee, if not below. They also had extra length in the shape of an absurdly generous species of hem, folded upwards and kept in position by buttons. The idea was that this could be lowered at night and tucked in gaiters or stockings, thus affording protection against mosquitoes. The effect in either position was acutely unbecoming, so much so that the trying-on of the issued garb occasioned a painful hilarity, like viewing the humiliation of an Oliver Hardy. Luckily, a fellow existed in one of the huts at Lee who for a trifling sum would remove the folded portions and hem the residue to a reasonable length. What remained was the inordinate width, that made sitting down in the garment, in company where modesty was desirable, as tricky as one imagines a similar operation to be in a short skirt. Unlike the padre, I do not think we ever wore our topees, except in jest. They were white, extremely large, and could only be transported in one's baggage by being saved for the last item in the kit-bag, the crown protruding like the top of an egg. The way to the Far East must have been littered with them, but I do not recall when I got shot of mine: because of thrift and respect for authority it was probably one of the last to go.

On the morning of 29 April, through a slight haze, a line of hills came into view ahead, clouds shrouding their tops. Nearer, it could be seen how they stretched backwards, very humped, patched with bottle-green vegetation, sprouting an occasional tree – the convoy floating towards them on a dead calm sea. Already there was an indication of immoderate depth in the landscape, so characteristic of Africa. As Margery Perham noted in one of her remarkable books about the continent, 'what a new value the green of earth offers after weeks at sea!' Over and above this was the scalp-crawling sensation conferred by the first sight of Africa itself – part of the modestly nude shoulder of an exciting figure of dreams or literature.

We anchored in Freetown harbour, little of the port discernible from our distance. In the hills were fragile-looking houses half hidden by the green that at the water ended in a brief, paint-box-bright sandy-red cliff of soil. Soon the ship was the focus of activity, a commonplace to tropical voyagers: to us, who but for the war would for ever have been locked in temperate lands, a novelty. A one-seater canoe, like a wood splinter, came far below to the ship's side, the negro guiding it with a closed-umbrella-shaped paddle, singing 'Hallelujah, I'm a bum' and 'Ippy-I', and calling for 'Glasgow tanners' and a pipe. Whether his shrewd appeal to nationalist sentiment overcame traditional closeness was not clear. He was the first of a succession of such, prepared to dive for the sixpences, even pennies; bringing bananas for sale. Some on board did business, dubbing the visitors 'Charlie', asking what time they signed on at the 'Labour', enquiring lasciviously after their wives. The visitors' insolence was not concealed by a mock naivity, and I reflected ruefully that their idiomatic phrases had been picked up from many boat-loads of the only theoretically more civilized and free. A serious exchange, obviously initiated by a socialist like myself, revealed that one canoist worked on the jetty at Freetown – night duty, 5 p.m. to 5 a.m., wages £2. 10s a month. A persistent memory of the port: a negro in the water, his chip of a boat near him, the green hills behind, calling through a mouthful of pennies: 'Any mo'? Any mo'?'

The few days' halt at Freetown seemed to consolidate the decline in fortune and volition, even then not awfully high, initiated by the news of one's drafting to Ceylon. The heat blistered the brow, seized up the bowels: the brilliant light, exhilarating at first, soon produced an acute headache. I told in *The Perfect Fool* of the speeches after an evening concert, when the captain of one of the escorting cruisers earned crashing applause with bloodthirsty anti-Jap sentiments, and the captain of the *Capetown Castle* announced that he would go down with the red ensign flying rather than be captured. More applause, rather less thunderous. This really not surprising manifestation was oddly depressing: a sharper case of the kind exemplified by the future Lord Martonmere starting to sing the National Anthem at my peace meeting in the Thirties, as related in *Vamp Till Ready*. It seemed as though one forgot, until so reminded, that a great part of mankind was engaged in putting its nationalistic and aggressive feelings into practice. The sentiments voiced, however, were far more lowering than the accompanying hints of perils attendant and to come, hints augmented by the thump of depth charges during the night, a German submarine rumoured to have penetrated the harbour defences. Troubled by what in my youth had been called 'heat spots' (and soothingly anointed with vinegar), I lay on my bunk scratching, and thinking horribly: 'I, shall never come back.'

Utterly characteristic of the ambivalence in myself about the men (and in the men about the state of the world) was the long political and social discussion in our 'flat' quite accurately reported in *The Perfect Fool*, recalling the nobility and pathos of some of the figures of the 'Loose Group', debating arena of my provincial youth. It need hardly be said that in 1942 the widespread desire for change and amelioration, coupled with some uncertainty about methods and results – mood underlying the overwhelming Labour vote in 1945 – was plainly evident. This was greatly to my taste, if insufficiently revolutionary.

We left Freetown on 3 May. The ship's food, never much to write home about, had degenerated vilely a week out of Liverpool. After Freetown it was not merely unpalatable but uneatable. The rich, including myself, lived on issue bread and butter, and sweet stuff from the canteen. No wonder, to harp on the topic, bowels were in indifferent order. Then the canteen ran out of chocolate and later biscuits. Organization was bad, commands stupid; both effected by boorish and bumptious Army and Marine Sergeants. Distress was all the greater for one trained in the standards of H.M.S. *Ganges*.

Mention in the journal of the bread seems to indicate that its quality was maintained. (Even in those days I was a bread freak, less arduous an enthusiasm even during the war than it became afterwards: much could be written on my postwar metropolitan quest for good bread). Very early in the voyage Willie Robertson had come up to me with serious expression and instructed me to look through a window in an edifice erected on deck. He said: 'They're working like niggers in there.' When I put my head in I saw a busy bakehouse, staffed mainly by blacks. It was typical of Willie, enhanced by his accent and timing that were characteristic of Scottish music-hall performers like Harry Lauder, Will Fyffe and, in a later day, the marvellous Renée Houston. Willie's presence was a great consolation. Not from him emanated anything spiritually or physically off-putting, though his appearance at times was apt to become bizarre, frequently (as in my grandfather's case) deliberately so (among the photographs to be mentioned later is one of him at what must be Port Reitz, wearing a flying-helmet and gumboots, with a revolver stuck in the belt of his khaki shorts). Many of us had requested and been granted permission to cease shaving, and quite soon Willie's pale, rather large, flat countenance was transformed by a heavy beard much more ginger than his hair, which was in fact strongly inclined to fair, wavy and parted near the middle.

> And Aflatun and Aristu
> Let their Beards grow, and their Beards grew
> Round and about the mainmast tree
> Where they stood still, and watched the sea.

Flecker's stanza was not wholly applicable, for my own whiskers grew patchily, even less comprehensively than those of the tennis star, Borg, and when they came to be inspected by the Lieutenant i/c the Naval draft I had to agree with him that they would never do.

Willie's tall, slightly leaning, shambling figure was not suited – whose was? – to pusser's khaki shirts and shorts. Nor was his appearance improved by his almost always wearing the kapok-filled life-jacket issued on boarding, an object that got grubbier as the voyage progressed since it had always to be at hand and was universally in use as a pillow when crashing one's swede on deck. Many Naval ratings kept their khaki shorts up with the blue webbing belt in use with serge bell-bottoms: Willie providently carried his enamel mug about, his belt threaded through its handle. Mugs had been issued with the life-jackets, and proved to be the more vital equipment. If *The Perfect Fool* is to be believed, my own mug was filched at an early stage, due to assuming the honesty of fellow draftees, typical sentimentality of the bourgeois Marxist of the time. How I replaced it is now mysterious; perhaps theft in my turn.

I have the feeling that Willie also wore the inflatable, motor-cycle-tyre-like lifebelt issued to all naval personnel as part of their initial kit, but this may only have been at critical moments or, even, a joke on his part, or the lingering memory of a facetious suggestion by me. His concern for his safety, if mined or torpedoed, and comfort, so far as concerned mugs of tea, was quintessentially characteristic, though that side of his persona, superficially self-centred and unheroic, did not seem dominant in my eyes, or at any rate induced only fond teasings. He was one to whom good jokes were told (though probably he filtered out the dross), and who himself invented many. His sensitivity to harm through warlike action was not paralleled by lack of boldness in his relations with authority. He had actually officially requested to be taken off the Ceylon draft, on the ground that his wife would be upset at his going. (At the time we regarded this as typical Williesque super cool cheek, but years after it came home to me that in truth he was thinking not of himself but his missis). And his calm bearding of a high railway official will be seen later. Like many Scots, certainly then, he had a civilian occupation connected with the sea, so prompting him to opt for the R.N., though calling-up as a writer (originally intended, as in my own case) would have made his previous experience more useful, for he had worked behind the counter in a shipping line's passenger division.

One afternoon, three days away from Durban, a couple of explosions, separated by ninety minutes or so, interrupted the solo-whist-playing of an afternoon watch off duty. I did not hear the first, but went on deck to see smoke proceeding from a depot ship that for some time had been on our starboard bow, the vessel already aft, and turning out of the convoy. The second explosion caused a similar happening to a merchant ship, which some said they could see settling down by the bows as we left her behind. The leisurely pace of catastrophe, often remarked on, was noticeable here. After the first explosion everyone grabbed their kapok life-jackets, suddenly transformed, like neglected, ugly creatures in fairy tales. On deck I encountered Willie. Surely this was an occasion when he had doubled up in life-jackets.

It must be borne in mind that rumour assigned various causes to these events, including mere boiler explosions, though two on the same afternoon seemed excessive. Perhaps it was not until the second that Willie and I arranged that if only one of us survived he would report to the other's wife. The precise nature of the report was not laid down. I would say Willie's nonchalance was less evident than my own, but courage properly so called was not put to any sort of test. On my part, superficial flippancy, the compulsion to joking or facetiousness in the face of the serious (all devices, perhaps, to keep hidden or protected the essential self) still operated. (Mines were almost certainly to blame, one heard later).

As a matter of fact, the moment of greatest unease of the voyage is related more or less verbatim in *The Perfect Fool*. Wandering through the ship, I came across a relatively uncrowded bathroom used by sergeants and the like. I say 'wandering', but it sticks in my mind that the exploration was specifically to discover such a wash-place, probably having observed vestiges of it in the shining faces and shirt-sleeved state of certain senior N.C.O.s. The *Capetown Castle* had a strong resemblance to the ship in which Karl Rossman is voyaging at the start of Kafka's *America*, particularly as to the parts cut off from the ordinary experience of passengers in the lowest class. After the war, when I read Brian Aldiss' S.F. novel *Non-stop*, about an enormous and labyrinthine space-ship, another literary parallel presented itself. In the *Capetown Castle*, the quest for lavatorial facilities was spurred by the water being turned on, in the crude troops' 'ablutions' erected on deck (like the bakehouse), only for two brief periods *per diem*.

I used the discovered bathroom quite regularly, though never without qualms, relying on the unfamiliarity of Army and Air Force Sergeants with the R.N. to avoid challenge. The F.A.A. draft was so small that the chance of encountering a suspicious senior naval N.C.O. seemed quite a long shot. My ploy was to go to the bathroom in shirt (collar removed) and trousers, the implication being that I was a Petty Officer, comparative youth accounted for by some technical skill with sonar or the like that had brought early promotion. A few faces actually became familiar enough to nod to. For my rule-respecting nature and fear of disgrace, the peril was substantial, detracting somewhat from the luxury of washes and shaves not queued for and in relatively comfortable surroundings.

After a visit one night, exploring curiously as in that novel does the hero of *Non-stop*, I found a small room, empty, containing a bath. I slipped in, bolted the door. In the linen dolly-bag issued at *Ganges* for toilet articles I had a cake of salt water soap bought with blind forethought from the ship's canteen. The great taps soon filled the commodious bath with sea-water. Lying in it, my nude body seemed already at the mercy of the greater saline element outside the ship. The squeakings and blowings from the timbers and vents round me were far from reassuring; the ambiguous trousers and shirt on the adjacent floor seemed a protection lost.

Submarines could be visualized, floating below the ship even as one floated in the itself floating ship. This was before the incident of the mines, otherwise they would have been added to the dangers conjured up, not the least of which were an inability to unbolt the door in case of alarm, and authority hammering on it, demanding an account of my trespass.

The protagonist of *Non-stop* even has my first name:

Forwards was a region like none Roy Complain had seen before. The grandeur of Sternstairs, the cosy squalor of Quarters, the hideous wilderness of Deadways, even the spectacle of that macabre sea where the Giants had captured him – none of them prepared him for the *differentness* of Forwards.

A taste of 'Sternstairs' came on my way to the concrete and iron tub when I had to pass, even penetrate, the sun-deck, where, as soon as weather permitted, stood a comfortable green-canvas chair with the Adjutant's name stencilled on it: MAJOR GORDON-WILSON. More commonplace deckchairs also appeared, for, so far as could be discerned by a denizen of 'Deadways', officers and such female supernumeraries as F.A.N.Y.S. lived under many of the conditions of a peace-time voyage – charming dining-room, cabins, barber's shop, games deck, gramophones, drink. At Freetown, a homosexual R.A.F. officer, previously noted as occasionally wandering, shyly smiling, on the poop deck, actually appeared in chic blue and white checked shirt and blue linen trousers. A few close friendships, outwardly discreet, were almost from the voyage's start formed among the troops themselves.

Senses were deranged, dreams all the more amazing, through keeping watch. The journal records an instance – getting only half an hour's sleep before being shaken to keep the middle-watch, and in the gun-post, under the Milky Way, snatches of half-sleep, stream of consciousness active as Mrs Dalloway's. I must have fallen into a deeper doze just before four, because marines roused me at twenty past, coming late on relief watch. I went down, undressed and wrapped myself in my blanket – the weather had cooled, approaching the Cape. I lay facing the wall behind the bunk which, being part of the ballroom, was veneered. Before I fell asleep I observed an ornamental strip of veneering of different grain: in sleep this became a silver cinema screen on which it seemed I could project any image I wished. Girls were running, scene from some mysterious scenario. I willed a more lascivious view but the result was fragmentary and soon faded. I was conscious the whole time of the folds of grey blanket round my shoulders: indeed, I could see them. Then I dreamed I was paralysed, with such accompanying alarm I decided to wake myself. I did so, or dreamed so, but stayed paralysed still – only able, cocooned in a blanket, to move my limbs a fraction.

There was a final dream, involving my mother, who confessed to me she had a cancer. I pleaded with her to go to London to see a specialist: 'What's the use of money if you die?' Rereading these few lines of the journal still brings unease, for seven years later she did die and from carcinoma. The strange anticipation undoubtedly arose from the long years of her undiagnosed hyperthyroidism – her resultant ill-health an anxiety deeper than my polite uncommun- icativeness, even our sharing of jokes, would indicate. (Doubtless, too, in the background of the dream was my father's illness and death, more than twenty years before, from the same disease). So now – I mean in the epoch when I write these words – chronology becomes painfully confused when I dream of her as still alive and suffering, as she grievously did, from that terminal malady, and, waking, I am momentarily unsure whether in truth she is dead or not.

On this voyage I seem to have written only two poems, the last in the collection *The Middle of a War*, one of them actually arising out of the favourable conditions for dreaming, especially gloomily, provided:

> I dreamed of my child's face, all bloody.
> Waking, I heard
> The tortured creak of wood, the whistling
> Like some night-haunting, death-presaging bird . . .

Alun Lewis, making a similar trip later the same year, did rather better, perhaps helped by material conditions, for by then he was commissioned. Though treating of some of the piddling matters mentioned in the foregoing pages, his 'A Troopship in the Tropics' achieves a certain detachment, the emotion recollected in tranquillity quality usually requisite for verse of any value. And one of his trooper poems became quite famous: 'Song: On seeing dead bodies floating off the Cape.' What luck my own was not among them.

2.   The Clique

I asked him once about the excitements of warfare . . . He said: 'It was like waiting for a train at Mullingar.'

– Padraic Colum: Preface to Stephen MacKenna's *Journal and Letters*

As we came into the harbour at Durban there was a stout woman in white on the quay singing patriotic and nostalgic songs to us through a megaphone, though the time was not yet 7 a.m. She was said to be there to greet every troopship; perhaps had done so since the Boer War. The sense returned of being at the mercy of history, history written in a style one strongly disapproved of, even though playing an evidently important role – the pervading sense when lugging hammocks about on Aintree station under the eyes of history's nonentities. Having been denied it at Freetown, everyone expected shore-leave here, watch and watch about. But at 9.30 a.m. orders came to pack, and we were all off the *Capetown Castle*, with our kit, by 11 a.m. We entrained at the dock, and in another hour had moved off to a transit camp, Clairwood, by the racecourse, six miles or so out of Durban.

Establishments placarded DUNLOP, LEVER BROS., and STANDARD OIL were passed on the way, confirmation we were here to defend those monopolist interests and only incidentally to defeat the evil Axis powers. My complete lack of patriotic or straight-forwardly anti-fascist sentiment (as confirmed at the ship's concert) was personally characteristic, and possibly others were in like case. I daresay the attitude rose partly from feeling that keeping quiet about disagreeableness might postpone its effect indefinitely – rather as I used to smile with my lips closed as a boy to hide the

15

fact that an eye tooth, growing out like Dracula's, needed dental attention. Even the sparse journal entries show that I still saw the world through innocent left-wing eyes. On the railway line to Clairwood, I noted, on one side were the 'suburbanish pretty residences of the well-off: on the other the corrugated hovels of the Indians.'

The last word indicates my initial confusion about the different colours of skin. I could not tell which were the country's indigenous inhabitants, which the immigrants (or their descendants) from the Indian sub-continent, the business being further complicated by the 'coloureds', a category of mixed breeds and varying complexions. Needless to say, the racial barriers reinforced by the authorities (extending even to the use of the public benches along the seafront) were greatly displeasing, and during all my time in Africa I gained virtuous pleasure by yielding the privilege of using facilities marked 'Whites (or Europeans) Only' – or, to put it more accurately, enjoyed mucking in where possible with non-whites. The influx of proletarian or proletarianised servicemen must have been a measurable liberalizing influence in African racial divisions, though without effect in the final crunches. The mere sight of whites engaged in menial tasks was surely an eye-opener to many non-whites.

Clairwood Camp, a town of tents pitched on a gentle hillside, overlooked a landscape through which I might have been driven by Richard Flower on our pre-war circuits of the Kent and East Sussex courts. The first meal eaten was tea: on the tables were newly-broached two-pound tins of preserves. By moving round, in the style of the Mad Hatter's tea-party, it was possible to sample half-a-dozen or so varieties, which I did, greedy after the lousy grub of the *Capetown Castle* – even trying out such dubieties as tomato jam. To South African marmalade, almost invariably excellent, I have stayed faithful to this day.

In Clairwood, the Proustian or Dickensian view of life's mechanics prevailed: one not only re-encountered men who had been on other drafts at Lee, but also those not seen since *Ganges* days. The final pages of *Copperfield*, say, were brought to mind. There was a strong buzz that the last two Ceylon drafts had been cancelled and made 'miscellaneous'; that is, available for any place, any vessel. A survivor from H.M.S. *Hermes* said the Japs 'had knocked shit out of' Trincomalee. It occurred to me that Durban might now be the Fleet Air Arm base, instead of a port farther east, but really

16

this seemed mere wishful thinking. One was fervent in one's hope of being saved, after all, from Ceylon – not because of Ceylon's contiguity to Japanese aircraft but simply because Ceylon was about the most distant place from home one was likely to get to. The farther from home, so it seemed, the less the chance of returning before the end of the war. Even moving up the African east coast, as I soon did, was a welcome step in the right direction, though the Mediterranean – Suez Canal route, which would have made it so in reality, was then unusable. How strange it now seems to have measured the sense of separation simply as the crow (or nightingale rather) flies.

There were seven to a tent: agreeable companions in mine, some old acquaintances. But despite the warm sunny days the clayey sand struck chill into the bones at night and got into all one's possessions. Astounding, after three years of the British black-out, to see lights shining under moon and stars. The roadways and alleyways between tents were illuminated by lamps on poles. Crowds of sailors, soldiers and airmen shuffled to and from the canteen, as in some emblematic scene, perhaps from Bunyan. In the long grass at the sides of the road cicadas chirped, loud enough to pain the eardrums. Beer in the canteens was strong and gassy, one shilling (5p) the pint bottle: on that first night we left the canteen quite early to giggle, smoke the dreadful cigarettes available ('Cavalla', one shilling and threepence for thirty six), and try to achieve comfort and sleep on the cold earth. But apart from the cicadas, the occasional locust or immense flying beetle, strange plant or tree, and a few other oddities, it was really like being in camp in the U.K. Among the oddities (so the journal found) was a young Javanese sailor (Royal Netherlands Navy) seen in the showers: skin *café-au-lait*, touches of black where in a 'European' would be touches of pink. What one found exotic very much illustrated the insulation during the Twenties and Thirties of the ordinary middle-classes not only from 'abroad' but also from the extensive visual material now a commonplace – just as one had no notion until the coming of the talkies at the end of the Twenties of the hideousness of American speech.

I think Clairwood was choreless and one was free to go into Durban every afternoon and evening. As in higher South African society, the shitty jobs, e.g. in the godown kitchens, had to be assigned to black labour. With typical enterprise, Willie had brought with him his box-Brownie camera, and several snapshots of the camp survive. One is of Willie and me with such a kitchen in the background, but I am sure we were mere bystanders, without menial or even supervisory duties – indeed, I have a book under my arm. Before sending the snapshot home, I wrote on the back: 'SIR THOMAS LIPTON AND FRIEND.' Though we are unglamorously garbed in singlets and Number Two trousers, our taxi-drivers' caps are upgraded somewhat by white cap-covers (later to be made familiar in England by their retention by those returning from abroad, not displeased thus to proclaim their foreign service). The cap and his distinguished beard give Willie the fanciful resemblance to the rich, yacht-racing grocer – evidently still remembered though dead a dozen years. It was in Clairwood Willie said: 'Come and watch this. They're baffled.' He took me over to a few black camp-employees, for whom he then performed some simple but adroit trick with coins, the sort of feat he had a useful supply of, like his jokes. Hard to say whether he or his audience were the more amused. The pleasure he took was the kind he would have got from the puzzlement of children. He was not at all left-wing, but always put himself imaginatively into the position of the underdog, uninhibited, for example, about expressing – to whites – his outrage at racial discrimination.

To a puritan lefty from wartime England, Durban seemed a city of over-ripe and almost embarrassing luxury. Ice-cream, fruit, clothes, cigarettes, chocolate – rationed or scarce in England – were plentiful at pre-war prices. All the books, cosmetics, fountain-pens, watches and cameras, equally plentiful, seemed to be imported – 'a great plantation,' I noted, 'where the Whites live on the backs of the Indians and natives and drive about in great high-powered American cars.' The depth of thought may be measured by the level of the prose. Everything appeared to me, appropriately, in black and white – the headdresses of the Zulu ricksha drivers, elaborate but shabby, and a frail, diminutive Indian boy selling C.P. pamphlets in a pub. But one had to accept, as simple bonuses to various senses, brandy (at least that was domestic) at ninepence a nip; the Durban Symphony Orchestra; and the Durban girls, perennially tanned and summer-frocked. Curious that I cannot remember the name of the then permanent conductor of the D.S.O. – Edward somebody? – rather a dandy, held his baton between the first and second fingers of his loosely-clenched right hand, waved it swimmingly about a good deal but never dropped it.

We had docked at Durban on 18 May 1942. The weeks went

by, with various buzzes about the eventual fate of the Ceylon draft. We had a 'casual' pay parade, but on such occasions the amount doled out was always meagre, the service over-anxious to ensure that no man's account was in the red. I must have departed from England with a decent supply of cash, for there was no time for Kate to have arranged bank withdrawal facilities for me in South Africa. Not that I needed, or had the resources for, substantial drawings, and when pay came regularly the fact that I made the minimum allotment to Kate left me better off than most, anyway. Exiguous pay and the availability of Durban brought ruin to some. From Leading Air Fitter (was he an electrician? the knowledge has gone with the D.S.O. conductor's surname) Goodbody I bought a cheap watch even cheaper than the price he had paid. I did not really want it (though may possibly have thought it, in the manner of Caton of the Fortune Press, as related in *Vamp*) 'good stock' – for I had myself bought a watch in Durban, despite possessing a perfectly sound one already. It may well have been I envisaged a grotesque future when watches would be effective currency, as indeed happened in the warring nations eventually on the losing side. Goodbody was one of the seven in the tent – smallish, black hair well brilliantined down but still in parts unruly, and possessing a true 'tiddley suit' (doeskin, double-breasted, gold badges) which (now I come to think of it) may well have encouraged him to visit Durban more frequently than his current resources warranted. A mild, companionable character, how vivid his appearance and slightly salivated speech still is – yet I cannot recall him after Clairwood.

Even when what seemed definitive news arrived on 10 June that we were to move on the morrow, no destination was named. Kitbags, hammocks, green suitcases, toolboxes, were lugged to the roadway where the cicadas chirped in the sunshine. The end of a summer holiday was the situation evoked. On 11 June, in Durban harbour, we went aboard a nasty, rusty, quite small craft, said to have been condemned before the war, called the *Manela*. With the fraternal instinct seemingly possessed by all Hibernians, Willie found on the forecastle a fellow Scot, crew member, a fat cook, cleaning baking tins he said had been unused for fifteen years. I wonder whether at the time one saw in this encounter (rather more in the coming Ealing style than that of the war documentary) any connection with the submarine assault and consequent chronic Allied shipping shortage. Willie's business experience enabled him to ask a pertinent question apropos *Manela*: 'Is she a guid sailing ship?' 'Anything but thaat,' said the cook. 'It's a wonder she's no moving the noo.' We were, of course, still at the quayside.

Our mess deck, a forward hold, was not too horrible, given the *Manela's* outward aspect. What might be deemed a reasonable number was aboard to use the long tables and benches. Theoretical negative features were being on the waterline, and my assigned ammick hooks on the wrong side of the vessel's permanent list. In the corner was a rat-trap: *per contra*, a blanket had been laid on the deck for a fine cat with two charming kittens. We sailed the following day for Mombasa, alone, unescorted. Lieutenant Bailey, the officer in charge of the R.N. draft, said he would not know our next port of call until we had left Mombasa to go to it, but he thought it would not be in Ceylon. To this touch of Sutton Vane's *Outward Bound* was added a tincture of Conrad. Rolling like Mae West, the *Manela* hugged the coast, mostly high ivory dunes topped with silver-green vegetation, broken occasionally by a flattish piece like a golf-course; of human habitations not a sign. On the after well-deck were a few mangy hens. The crew looked surly and villainous, was said to suffer desertions at every port, and therefore paid well in arrear. There must have been a library of a kind on board, for the journal reports me reading *Henry Esmond* and other works I would never have bought. Thackeray was just the sort of author thrifty patriots took from their shelves to give to the fighting services and merchant navy: I recall elsewhere trying to read *Pendennis*. Print-starved though I was, Thackeray proved a tough nut, has always remained so: a pity I did not come to him through his early works.

Lieutenant Bailey was regular Navy, admirable example of pre-war selection and training: smart, forthcoming, concerned to secure the greatest benefit possible for the ratings in his charge. Would I have put this view in such terms at the time? I had sympathy for non-commissioned regulars, but class prejudice may have made me grudging about others. Also, it must not be forgotten there was a category of officers known as 'Naval pigs'. After just over a week's voyaging, the *Manela* docked at Mombasa – low green coast, white, red-roofed villas, a concealed harbour containing (*inter alia*) *Indomitable* and *Royal Sovereign*. With commendable speed Lieutenant Bailey announced that, however improbable it seemed for naval personnel, we were bound for Nairobi, where a naval air station was being created. All were greatly chuffed at the prospect of this cushy number, except a dozen or so of sterner stuff – perhaps regulars, like the efficient Bailey – who volunteered for carriers. The next afternoon, a Sunday, we had shore leave after divisions in whites. If blue fore-and-aft rig made one resemble a taxi driver (of those days), white fore-and-aft transformed one into a steward or barman, though once ashore one could illegally unhook the jacket's high collar and so make a pretence of more-becoming reveres. Walking along a tarmac road from the oil dock where we were berthed to the town, the ambience changed from Conrad to Graham Greene. About that first afternoon in East Africa I made what for me was a quite long journal entry. I am surprised by the prescience that led me to end by noting the 'hopeless air' hanging over everything: 'what one thinks is let's get out and leave the mess for the natives to clear up as best they can.' I never lost this puzzlement about British East Africa (as I think it was still commonly called). Surely the white landowners could never be persuaded to give up power in Kenya: indeed, they were demanding more. It seemed inevitable that the astute Asians throughout the territory would continue as an entrepreneurial class at all levels, and that educating, financing and energizing the black to enable him to compete with the other races was certainly very long-term, if not utopian. All seen in Mombasa led to this view.

At first, the local colour seemed merely daubed on something not far from a basic English suburbanization of the inter-war period: concrete, corrugated   iron, petrol-filling stations. But despite the newness and the colour (red fez, rich vegetation, bright saris) squalor was pervasive. As we had addressed the bum-boat navigators on the other side of the continent, so the Asian owners of the open-fronted wooden shops impudently hailed us as 'Charlie'. Everything seemed dear, even the carved wooden tourist objects displayed by blacks on the pavements. At the 'East' end of the main street was an incredibly decrepit house labelled 'Jaurina Hotel', outside which a few patriarchs sipped tea from saucers, an intimation I fear I did not fully exploit when I came to invent the 'Hotel Splendide' for my boys' adventure novel, Savage Gold. On a few walls were tattered little posters: BE INNOCULATED AGAINST YELLOW FEVER – but who could read or act on them, who knows?

Even in the brief time available there were the usual service scares that some were not to go to the sanctuary of the Kenya highlands. What amazing luck it seemed, therefore, when I found myself on the Monday following the Saturday announcement one of the 'advance party' of ten detailed to go to the Nairobi Civil Aerodrome. It was said the Fleet Air Arm had taken over the aerodrome as Middle and Far East maintenance depot; scarcely credible panic station following the Japanese bombardment of Trinco – a sort of last-stand eyrie, so it seems now, such as the Nazis planned to make Berchtesgaden. Seats on the ordinary train leaving Mombasa at 4.30 p.m. had been booked for the advance party, its own differences of rank extinguished by the local compulsion for all whites to travel similarly. One played a strange brief charade of pre-call-up life as red-fez'd, white-gowned, bare-footed stewards served dinner in the dining-car, thereafter put up couchettes with snowy linen in the compartment. Before the early equatorial night fell the long train could be seen chugging upwards through dramatic forest land; by morning the compartment window framed grassy highland plains with their herds of game and immense skies, soon to become utterly familiar.

The aerodrome seemed merely some tin and wooden huts along a tarmac road leading nowhere. A few hangars subsequently disclosed themselves. The airfield consisted simply of a portion of the Athi Plains, I think already a game reserve. I do not recall a perimeter fence: in any case, such as ostrich and gazelle were quite close at hand. The D.F. (Direction Finding) and some other fitters were assigned to the 'Special W/T Section', cognomen masking, as at Lee, the secrecy of radar. The locale consisted of a hangar, with store, small test-shop and office. The work was not simply repairing aircraft radar sets but also effecting the necessary airframe modifications to enable aircraft actually to be fitted with radar. Such was the novelty of the device in the F.A.A. in June 1942.

Though my journal was soon to peter out, I have a page or two about the situation and leading personalities in the Special W/T Section. When I wrote *The Perfect Fool* early in the Sixties I added to this what strike me now as authentic additional memories, though of course in the novel there is artistic compression, and conversations that could not have been accurately recalled. Historical truth is further complicated by the existence of a separate sheet I now find folded between the pages of the journal – a sheet containing the start of a short story about the Section which I undoubtedly wrote immediately following the events dealt with. Though the five or six hundred words of the story are naturalistic, they have a lurking Kafkaesque air which may well have thickened had I proceeded with the fiction.

As I write, I wonder about the reason for this mild obsession with the Section. It could perhaps be ascribed to the fact that thus far my life in the Navy had been all training and toing and froing: this was my first proper job. Certainly one was struck by, say, the familiar A.S.V. units laid out in the unfamiliar setting of the test-shop – the bumping pitch and leather ball after the smooth concrete and rubber ball of the playground. In *The Perfect Fool* the hero speculates as to whether certain persecutory items are not mere paranoia on his part, a touch of the Gilbert Pinfolds. One or two incidents still remain ambiguous in my mind, though the fundamental cast of *that* is to regard its owner as possessed of solid common sense, free from fantasy. So it may be of interest to reproduce parts of the three stages of the record, adding a curious postlude of many years later.

My journal has the following – amazingly feebly written, no wonder the entries soon lapse:

Thursday 24 June.   We are sent to the D.F. place . . . We had not been there a couple of hours before there was a ROW. The place is run by a Lieutenant (apparently a nonentity), a Sergeant, a P.O., and two leading hands – one in the hangar, one in the test-shop. The hangar one the type I hate, blond, tiptilted nose, big nostrils, had already made himself fairly objectionable by giving us directions ('two of you will work in the hangar, two in the shop') which he had no authority to give and which proved to be (as I anticipated) all nonsense. Coming back from stand-easy I wandered into the shop and turned-up nose told me to take a ladder back to the hangar. I stared at him. 'Why don't you take it back yourself?' He said, 'I'm telling you to take it back.' I said, 'Who are you? A P.O.?' I had on me my reckless bad-tempered mood – rare but satisfying – my shyness and so on swamped by anger. We had a little argument. 'I'm a leading hand – the same as you.' 'Yes, but when were you rated?' 'That has nothing to do with it.' At last I wandered off, feignedly intent on some errand. I heard and ignored his voice calling after me. Then the P.O., red and wrathful, took a hand. I said, 'If you say so that's another matter.' I moved the ladder with Barry. A little later we all fell in in the hangar and had a little pep talk by the P.O. who offensively told us who was who and what was what. He said, 'D.F. ratings are not *proper* leading hands – they are only rated to make their pay up.' This was a mistake because when he'd finished I challenged him and asked him what he meant by 'not proper leading hands.' A long argument and he climbed down. Afterwards in private he was as nice as pie . . .

Wednesday 8th July. Big nostrils is really the best of the hangar's ruling clique and we are now polite and amiable to each other. The P.O. (tall, insolent, vulnerable) is still offensive. The blond, anaemic workshop killick wears brass buttons and calls himself, entirely without justification, a P.O. He is aped by another blond, a cheerful vain extravert who tries to borrow money. In charge of the whole thing is a Wavy Navy Lieutenant, weak I imagine, white teeth and a minor public school voice – also blond. I think for my truculence I am being *victimised* e.g. a halfday stopped, told off for a job ten minutes before secure. This worries me not at all – lends some interest in fact to the long days with practically f. all to do. But not much interest. I have made myself an elegant paperknife out of aeroplane wire and so has everyone else . . . V. important in midst of real or imaginary 'persecution' and clique rivalries to preserve one's normal and proper character. This I find less difficult than I would a few years ago. I have a 'character' it seems, even though it consists mainly of intellectual snobbery. No, kindness stiffened by that.

The prose of the short story pulls the business together a bit. It starts with a paragraph about deliberately impeding a lizard on the hangar floor so as to cause it to shed its tail – an episode, so far as appears, unconnected with the 'clique', but perhaps of ultimate emblematic purport. The story then goes on:

The clique which controls the hangar is, now I come to think of it, blond. It has fair complexions and hair, dazzlingly golden hair, some of it. On my first day in the hangar I antagonized the clique and I cannot think that the clique will ever get over it. One of the clique, who is of the same rank as myself, told me to do a menial task he could and should have done himself. He caught me on my dignity and stubbornness and we stood opposite each other and argued. He was a little taller than me, blond, with a turned up nose and great vulgar nostrils. 'I asked you quite civilly,' he kept stupidly saying. In the end I walked away while he still ordered me. But my motion was arrested by an even taller blond, a Petty Officer of sulky, healthy and infantile aspect. He supported Turned Up Nose and was in a red-faced rage. Of course, in this situation, I carried out the menial task. Later the inhabitants of the hangar were assembled and harangued by the P.O. in a mock straight-from-the-shoulder manner. I took him up on something he said and he was practically forced to withdraw it. And so foolishly I presented myself quite falsely to the clique.

The clique could not exist without the connivance or lethargy of the officers. There is both connivance and lethargy. In charge of the section is a Lieutenant called Fagg, with a pink handsome face, closely-cut fair hair and a minor public school voice. So far he has never once spoken to me but I have heard him speak to others, almost always facetiously. I imagine him to be weak but his activities are hidden from me so I cannot really judge. It is clear, anyway, that he considers the best way to run the hangar is to have a clique – he is part of the clique, the members of which speak familiarly to him, even mere leading hands like Turned Up Nose. The other officer, the Pilot, is of little importance, but is amusing enough to be mentioned, and mentioning him does help slightly to communicate the atmosphere of the place. When he is not flying he very often plays practical jokes, like filling a paint spray with water and spraying Lieutenant Fagg. Or sometimes he makes a catapult out of a bracelet strip and a rubber band, and shoots paper pellets at people. His age must be between 25 and 30.

The hangar looks out across an immense plain.

Here the story breaks off. The Pilot (a character surely founded on actuality) had utterly gone from memory, as had the term 'bracelet strip', an item available from the store, common in effectuating the A.S.V. 'mods'. In *The Perfect Fool* the relevant episode also contains material I could scarcely have invented, but now forgotten. The narration here is in the third person, and 'Lieutenant Fagg' and the 'Pilot' form a composite persona. Or (it comes to me uneasily as I write) did I merely split it for the purpose of the short story? The question is not really settled by pondering the reunion I shall soon describe. I should add that in *The Perfect Fool* Willie Robertson appears as Duncan Cummings.

The hangar, with its accompanying store, workshop and office, was for the sake of security known as the 'Special W/T' section.

Here the four radar mechanics of the draft reported the day after their arrival. In the workshop a native with a broom was grunting a song and raising a cloud of dust. Along the wall were the radar sets they had come during their training to know so well, but in this place taking on a slightly alarming character of serious purpose. An air mechanic entered, apparently for the purpose of smoking a thin inch of cigarette and concealing an enamel mug behind a spare cathode ray tube. He had the specially nonchalant but knowing air of the expert in front of the tyro. Duncan Cummings asked him what happened at the morning stand-easy.

'A van comes round with tea and cakes. Red Cross it is. Some wizard birds on it sometimes.'

The negro sweeper and the air mechanic in due course disappeared, and the eventless, informationless boredom characteristic of so much service life settled on the workshop. Alan kicked an empty cardboard packing-case, and screamed.

'I wonder where the shithouse is,' mused Harry White, a comparatively elderly member of the party, with a bald patch and a big adam's apple, often scarred from shaving in bad lights.

'I wonder,' said Alan with unobserved irony.

At last a tall blond leading air fitter bustled momentarily in. 'Are you the draft?' he inquired needlessly. Harry White politely answered his questions.

'My name's Facer,' said the leading air fitter. 'I'm in charge of this test shop. I shall want two of you in here, and the other two will work in the hangar. Every aircraft on this station has to be modified for A.S.V., so there's a busy time ahead. No farting about.'

The fourth radar mechanic, a boy younger than the rest, looked suitably depressed. Duncan Cummings, sitting on his toolbox in the background, had started an air mail letter-card. Alan squatted on the floor by him and said: 'Dear Mother, It's a bastard . . . Dear Son, So are you.'

Harry White puffed at his pipe. 'I bet that bloke was talking tripe. I bet he has no say in where we have to go.'

Alan had been not unimpressed by Leading Air Fitter Facer, but now saw the weakness of what the man had said. 'Of course, we shall all work in the test shop. What the bloody hell have we been trained for?'

Nevertheless, by stand-easy, the Petty Officer of the Section, a youngish wireless operator, had told them all to work in the hangar. There, everything that went on seemed to Alan not only beyond any skill of his but also to require no assistance from outsiders. A rigger was sitting on the hull of a Walrus, bostiking an aerial; somebody was hidden in a cockpit of a Swordfish crooning and using an electric drill; while on the grassy plain in front of the hangar another Swordfish was having its aerials aligned. At a bench running along the back Alan found the Birmingham leading air fitter who had been on his watch in the trooper. He was industriously filing something in a vice, and Alan realized the gap that separated him from the genuine tradesman, who could so quickly find a niche for himself. He watched the operation for a while and then said: 'Is there anything for me to do, Archie?'

'Shouldn't think so, mate.'

'What the hell are you doing, then?'

'Making a paperknife.'

After stand-easy Alan and Harry White wandered back into the test shop, for as radar mechanics it seemed to be their only possible milieu. They discovered that Duncan had preceded them to continue writing his air-mail letter-card. The test shop also had the advantage of permitting smoking but Alan had scarcely lighted a cigarette when Leading Air Fitter Facer came in and said to him in casual tones: 'Take that ladder back into the hangar.'

It was only a momentary flicker of the eyes by which Alan confirmed to himself what he knew needed no confirmation – that there was merely a single anchor on Facer's shirt sleeve. 'Why don't you take it back yourself?'

'I'm telling you to take it back.' Facer's countenance had assumed a serious and determined look. He had one of those noses in which the nostrils are vertical instead of, as is usual, more or less parallel with the ground, so that Alan, confronting them across the tense three feet to which the distance between the opposed parties had been reduced, felt that it was only the gloom and vegetation of the cavities that prevented him from seeing deep into Facer's head.

'Who are you? A petty officer?' It seemed to Alan almost unfair for him to have ignored the command and to feel an anger that completely cancelled out his normal shyness and indifference, for Facer was pitiably powerless and out of order.

'I'm in charge of the test shop,' Facer said.

'That may well be, but you're only a leading hand, and I'm a leading hand. I'm just the same as you.'

'But when were you rated?' Facer asked. The feebleness inherent in the question was apparent even to him, for he dropped his eyes and pushed a bakelite tuning key to a place of greater safety on the test bench.

'That has nothing whatever to do with it.'

'Oh yes, it has.'

'Nothing at all,' said Alan, his light tone indicating a chivalrous reluctance to press his advantage home. There were few more exchanges of this infantile variety, and then it occurred to Alan that his allotted place was the hangar. Murmuring something not quite coherent about having a job to observe on the work bench, and even visualizing Archie Elliott's paperknife-making as a rational cause of his going, he turned his back on Facer and strolled out of the test shop. Facer's voice called after him, but Alan pressed on, stopping only in the middle of the hangar, when the voice had ceased, to watch conscientiously a mechanic screwing on the cap of an aerial bollard.

A minute later he was summoned to the test shop by the petty officer, red and wrathful. Alan said: 'Well, of course, if *you* say so . . .' He seized the ladder; Harry White came nobly to his help, and they bore it away. Before the morning ended the new radar mechanics were ordered to fall in in the hangar, where the petty officer, in offensive manner, told them superfluously who was in charge of what. And he added: 'You aren't *proper* leading hands, you know. You've only been rated up to make your pay up.'

At the end of the harangue, Alan said, in a voice that seemed to him to tremble too ludicrously for the question to be other than ignored: 'What do you mean, P.O., that we aren't "proper" leading hands?'

The petty officer strode up. Whether he had been flying or was going to fly that morning or whether he merely wore the thing to reinforce what he perhaps imagined his trade badge too modestly proclaimed, a flying-helmet lay softly in the nape of his neck, the Y lead from the earphones hanging on his chest with the appearance and indefinable authority of a stethoscope on a physician's. 'How long have you been in the Navy, Percival?'

'Fourteen months.'

'There you are. How can you be a proper leading hand in

that time? In peacetime a bloke waited seven years or more for his hook.'

It was not so much to establish his own position as to defend the educational and hierarchical system of the Navy that Alan proceeded to demolish this proposition of the petty officer's, for though he had been conscripted with no illusions about the Government's ideology and with a dread of a communal and perhaps painful life, once part of the Service he felt an indulgent respect for its laws and an irritated pity for its faults, as though for a parent. And it was a tribute more to the traditions of the Service rather than to Alan's persuasive powers that quite soon the petty officer – who was a regular serviceman – handsomely admitted that he should never have made his invidious differentiation between leading hands.

A not inconsiderable part of the petty officer's persona at first eluded Alan's identification (like those puzzle pictures designed for children to discover mistakes, where, for example, a hyena has been given a lion's head), and he imagined that the man's authoritative and impressive air was wholly a matter of character. Then he realized that the petty officer was wearing an officer's cap. On its band was sewn, of course, a petty officer's badge but the peak that projected below it was altogether more massive than the peaks of other petty officers' caps, and the crown was almost of a dinner plate amplitude. A third figure in the ruling clique of the 'Special W/T' section – an anaemic, red-eyed leading air fitter, regarded by the P.O., Facer and himself as the genius of the test shop – also affected an ambiguity of dress, but of less intimidating character than the P.O.'s cap, being merely a set of brass petty officer's buttons sewn on his bush jacket, in mild anticipation of a rating that was said to be coming through.

The initial encounter with Facer and the P.O. induced in Alan a sense of being oppressed, but a rearrangement of accommodation brought Facer into Alan's mess and the hazards of domestic existence made some sort of commerce inevitable. Hanging about the 'ablutions' early one evening waiting for the water to come on, Alan found himself next to Facer and could not help amiably remarking: 'Next to eatable food, the chief thing wanted on this station is a regular water supply.'

Facer agreed.

'Or perhaps before regular water a supply of bumf in the rears,' Alan said.

'As a matter of fact, I buy my own private supply in the town,' said Facer.

'Do you now?' Possibly there really was some ability in Facer.

Later, in the mess, he told Duncan Cummings of this evidence of Facer's resource. 'He's quite human,' Alan added generously.

'Aye.'

'Even P.O. Hind can be human. You'd be bad-tempered if you had to run that bloody "Special W/T" section.'

'Aye.'

'You don't sound convinced.'

Duncan turned round from the business of putting a cake, bought specially for the purpose at the morning's stand-easy, in the pocket of his jacket which hung on a nail, conveniently at his bed-head, so that returning later that evening from shore-leave in the town he would have something before going to sleep to appease his perpetual hunger. He said: 'I think they're all a lot of shits.'

'Linley's a shit, I dare say,' said Alan judiciously. Linley was the great radar brain, the anaemic air fitter of the test shop.

'They're a shower of Nazis. Have ye no' obsairved they're all blonds?'

It was true that Hind had a sandy quiff, Facer a fair brillian-tined cap, Linley floppy, waving golden locks, and the officer in charge of the section, the weak giggling pilot, struggling pale hairs round his premature baldness. 'You think they're an Aryan cell planted by Hitler in the British Navy? I see your point, Cummings, but don't you think their sabotage of the war effort is too crude for the Germans?'

'It's you they're sabotaging.'

'Me?'

'Today, for example, Hind gave you that Walrus job ten minutes before secure.'

'Well, somebody had to . . .'

'Then you had that half-day stopped.'

'Other people have had a half-day stopped. Haven't you heard there's a war on?'

'Yon Nazis are sabotaging you, Alan, and tha's a faact.'

Of course, when it was pointed out, Alan reflected afterwards, by a detached observer, one saw it at once. But it struck him that since his whole existence now was in a sense the result of victimization, a little more could scarcely hurt. Indeed, it added a faint interest to the long days spent in idleness or attempting work for which he was untrained and unfitted, to feel himself a marked man. Sometimes, seeing Hind's quiff, or the gargantuan peak of his cap, towering among some group in the hangar, or fascinated yet repelled by the open vistas of Facer's nostrils, a little area of hatred would boil in his stomach, but it quickly died down. It was not impossible, in fact, for him to find some facets of the clique to pity – Hind's manifest ambition, for example, trying to thrive on the deficiencies of his regular service background. Once or twice, lying contorted in an aircraft fusilage, grazing his knuckle by slipping with his screwdriver off the head of a screw or conceiving it utterly impossible to squeeze in the tray for part of the A.S.V. set in the position indicated by the mod. leaflet, he would rasp out some feigned sobbing quickly changing into consciously insane laughter, and he would see himself as part of a quite farcical world, where the machinations of a Hind or Linley were no more or less significant than the rhetorical speeches of a Churchill or the British disasters in the Far East.

On the bench at the back of the hangar he, too, occupied the hours by making himself a paperknife out of aeroplane wire. With the others, he kept his toolbox on the bench and never thought to leave it locked. When his round-nosed pliers and handiest screwdriver were missing he imagined he had left them in an aircraft and actually went out on the airfield and searched the interior of a Walrus made searingly hot by the morning sun. And then when he came to use his centre-punch he found it blunted. He had when a child, for years mistakenly thought that the soap always in use at his grandparents' was called *cold* tar soap, and at first he toyed with the idea that his conception of centre-punches having points was equally erroneous, that they served some completely other purpose. Then, rather more sensibly, it occurred to him that the centre-punch issued to him with the other contents of his toolbox was one of a batch of duds foisted off on the Navy by an unscrupulous contractor. It seemed mere paranoia to conclude that like the missing pliers and screwdriver, the mutilated punch was evidence of malice or hatred.

More than thirty years after the persecutory events in the 'Special W/T' section, my path through life once more crossed that of

'Lieutenant Fagg' (as I shall continue conveniently to call him). By that time I had been Oxford's Professor of Poetry, much publicity attending the notorious election, and was currently a Governor of the B.B.C. I had retired from being the Woolwich Equitable Building Society's solicitor, but was on its Board. One of the Society's Regional Managers told me that at a public dinner in a provincial city he had sat next to a local business tycoon who claimed to know me, had in fact had me under his command in the Navy. The name supplied by the Regional Manager rang no bells. In the light of what happened, it is not easy to recover the dubiety I had initially about the identity of this individual, though suspecting him to be the former supremo of the Special W/T Section. 'Is he blond?' I asked the Regional Manager. The answer was equivocal: the hair was sparse and greying.

At the public dinner an open invitation to the Regional Manager to bring me to lunch had been issued by Fagg (if indeed it were he), which I said I would take up if I found myself in the provincial city in question, as might well happen on B.B.C. or building society affairs. Some date thus conveniently occurring had to be cancelled by Fagg, and eventually I made a special journey, less to satisfy curiosity than to oblige the Regional Manager, who hoped for some business to accrue from Fagg's organization.

We were received in a manner befitting the guests of tycoonery, and given lunch in the former Lieutenant's office, butled by an attractive secretary – though only one pre-lunch drink was achieved, and no more than one bottle of Moselle uncorked. Afterwards, I said to the Regional Manager that this was typical of Lieutenant Fagg (the identity was settled on sight), but it must be conceded that in Nairobi I never tested his hospitality. Our previous relations were only briefly discussed. Fagg said he remembered me sitting on a coil of rope, writing a poem; the locale being a troopship bound for India. I said, as was the case, that I had never been to India. This did not seem to daunt him: in any case he was more interested in establishing the extent of his tycoonery than gassing about the remote past. I see now it is quite interesting that a normal character like Fagg should also have an unreliable memory.

His fallacious recollection brought back to mind that the clique was dispersed, later in that summer of 1942, by being largely drafted to the sub-continent, though its power had earlier been broken by the arrival of a new draft of personnel for the Special W/T Section, headed by two officers. The effect on my own life of this influx I will later relate.

3.   I.F.F.

Why I write such good books

– Nietzsche (chapter heading from *Ecce Homo*)

Before leaving England I had handed to John Lehmann, in his capacity as a director of the Hogarth Press, the typescript of a collection of poems called *The Middle of a War*. As related in my previous autobiographies, I had met John in 1937, at his initiative after I had sent poems to *New Writing*, and he had given me constant literary encouragement. I expect there were sufficient hazards to keep me on tenterhooks until the thing actually came off, but after the poems produced at Lee-on-the-Solent and Seafield Park I think John was firm in his wish to publish a book. As often happens with collections of verse, *The Middle of a War* struck a new note, such as it was, by containing no pre-war poems, those passing muster having been included in my first book, the 1939 Fortune Press *Poems*. Not to be recaptured now, though the sense must have been acute, is the anticipation of the improvement in status following graduation from a 'Fortune Poet' to a 'Hogarth Poet'.

On delivering the typescript I recall informing John where each poem had previously appeared and his noting the name of the periodical at the foot of the page. This exercise was for the benefit of Leonard Woolf, always cagey about books of verse, I expect particularly so in the case of a virtually unknown poet. Much later, John told me he had had to go through the typescript page by page with Leonard, the fact and status of periodical publication proving a greater allaying of Leonard's suspicions than any merit in the poems. It was agreed I should send John such candidates for the book as might be written after I set out for Ceylon, which I did. They probably only amounted to the last three in the book, one being 'The Dream', which John re-christened 'On the High Seas', a touching attempt to make me an 'active service' poet, in the manner rather of Lieutenant Fagg at a later date. It was also John's idea to divide the book, exiguous enough, into two parts – pre-service poems and service poems. This, however, may have been my compromise with his (or Leonard Woolf's) desire for the service poems to come first, as putting the more saleable goods at the front of the shelf, an arrangement I would have been much against – if nothing else, for offending chronology, one quality at least of any poet's output.

The book, its slenderness accentuated by the scruffy paper of wartime, must have been published in October 1942. The sequence of receiving a copy and seeing the reviews has gone from me, but I do particularly remember Desmond MacCarthy's 'World of Books' article in the *Sunday Times* of 24 January 1943. MacCarthy was one of the elderly pundits still dominating the book pages of the heavy Sundays (they were succeeded after the war by a race of young pundits, not such an improvement as might have been anticipated). Most of his article was devoted to *The Middle of a War* in terms essentially friendly, even if very much from the cautious standpoint of a consciously older and wiser generation. The cutting or copy, sent by Kate, came with other mail to the little hut where I was then working. It so excited me I had to go out and walk up and down for a spell. It must be remembered I had just turned thirty-one and that MacCarthy's was virtually my first public recognition in the 'world of letters' – a world in which I had been absorbed and tried to compete since boyhood. I should add that Stephen Spender's notice in *The Observer* was equally friendly.

Subsequently, Kate reported a letter she had had from my brother saying how pleased he was I was getting some of the attention I deserved. Of course, my brother knew something of my long strivings and his touching remark struck me as the expression of a tenable view. But I did not quite see the business thus, though discrimination may be difficult to convey in the tricky area of self-evaluation. I desired my verse to be strictly judged, and still not to be found essentially wanting, though all too aware of its deficiencies myself. Such desire has persisted, fulfilled by a mere handful of critics, the bulk merely attacking irrelevancies or following changing fashion.

No doubt most indifferently successful artists feel similarly. Even the great are not immune: reading Michael Millgate's excellent recent biography of Hardy, I was struck once again how many critics in his lifetime pointed out, and objected to, Hardy's 'pessimism', though his poetry is full of enjoyment of the world; this business riling Hardy to the end.

MacCarthy's and other notices sent the book into a second impression, but the shortage of reading matter, if not so acute as on the *Manela*, gave every English wartime book a good chance of success. Practically all the 'service' poems had been written under training, yet many reviewers commended the book for its novelty in giving a picture of service life – an indication of the pretty wholesale avoidance of the call-up by the better-known Thirties poets. Needless to say, I claim no personal virtue through the working on my particular destiny of the due and common processes of the epoch. As described in *Vamp*, they had a generally good effect on my verse; and I suppose on my status with reviewers. I noted in *Vamp* the ire of old Herbert Palmer when reviewing my first book: it would be churlish not to record that he made handsome amends in his notice of *The Middle of a War* in *John o'London's Weekly*. What a pity I never wrote to thank him for a generosity all the more selfless in face of my rudery, in the previous decade, about a book by him.

The hut to which some kind visitant to the Mailing Office had brought the letter with the startling MacCarthy review was a little apart from the hangar housing the Special W/T Section. It may have been specially built for its function, which was the servicing of the I.F.F. (Identification Friend or Foe) radar apparatus housed in naval aircraft. That apparatus was essentially a box of tricks that magnified and returned an incoming radar signal. It was triggered into action by the A.S.V. apparatus also housed in naval aircraft (the ocean 'search' radar already referred to), so that friendly aircraft showed up unmistakably on the A.S.V. screen.

With another leading air fitter, Bob Park, I moved into the I.F.F. business in the middle of August. The move coincided with the arrival of the new Special W/T draft, so presumably the former was a consequence of the latter. Bob was a stocky, agreeable, strong-minded but good-humoured Scot, known already, of course, but with whom I became close friends during our I.F.F. days. He was of the breed of Scot that makes a fearless and tenacious wing half-back, to use a now obsolete term. The 'iffy hut', as we came to call it, was nearly as incommodious as the class-leaders' cubbyhole at H.M.S. *Ganges*, described in *Vamp*, but in similar manner acting as a refuge. Having the key, Bob and I sometimes used it out of working hours, I for my part writing a few lines of verse as well as letters.

Previous to the I.F.F. move I had scarcely been employed, least of all on the work for which I had been so long and expensively trained. I and my trade were not alone in this. Like the hero of *The Perfect Fool* I had occasionally helped with the A.S.V. mods, crawling into parts of aircraft (mainly Swordfish, with a sprinkling of Albacore and Walrus) difficult of access, for the devisers of the mods had had to use often maniacal ingenuity to accommodate the various bits and pieces. Strange sensation when I first drilled a hole in the fuselage of a Walrus to take a bolt to hold a rack on which to fix an A.S.V. unit. Since the Walrus was amphibian, one almost envisaged it sinking as a result of one's amateur labours. At another juncture some of us had been loaned to the Ordinary W/T Section, not to work on W/T sets (of which in any case we were ignorant) but to provide unskilled labour for the erection of an aerial mast and construction of an aerial frame. And the journal records that at least one day was spent chipping paint off an old car being renovated for the clique to use on shooting trips, work for which I was better fitted through experience at Chatham Dockyard and Seafield Park, as readers of *Vamp* may recall. The idleness among dockyard mateys that had shocked me at Chatham was reproduced among the ratings in Nairobi.

What a relief from the stupifying boredom to get to the iffy hut! Bob and I knew nothing about the I.F.F. equipment, for the Lee radar course had never touched on it, but an I.F.F. test set, perhaps two, had suddenly become available, from which the I.F.F. circuit diagram could be seen and test procedures gleaned. Perhaps there was even a service manual. With the test set or sets came a good lot of unserviceable I.F.F. equipment, for no one seemed ever to have opened up the latter, either in Nairobi or the entire Eastern theatre. When the apparatus failed, it was simply replaced. We quickly became familiar with the range of common faults and carried out appropriate repairs, the saving in money and *matériel* most agreeable to my thrifty nature.

With the hut came a handcart to convey equipment to and from the aircraft dispersed on the Athi Plains. Pulling this vehicle made Bob and me even more like the working proprietors of some minuscule business, perhaps in the scrap line. However, we were saved from menial duties vis-à-vis the hut by the arrival every morning of an *askari*, probably a mere auxiliary, to sweep it out. He was quite elderly, sang a little melody to the rhythm of his broom. In a lull I whistled it myself, with an effect on him akin to Willie's conjuring, ignorant of my childhood experience of picking up tunes in Blackpool's 'Happy Valley'. After the momentary surprise he was greatly amused. Though he had no English and I only a few words of Swahili, it was plain that part of the joke was the ruling class adopting a bit of the culture of the oppressed. In Africa I found a good indigenous response to jokes, only a touch of mime or slight facial change being necessary to convey the jesting aspect of any matter in hand.

When we first arrived in Nairobi it was possible to share the services of a native who would launder one's gear, clean shoes, and suchlike, at a price within the means even of leading hands. Willie and I had a stake in a young man called Edward. He spoke, or at any rate understood, some English, and wore a long-sleeved pullover and wristwatch – too sophisticated for Willie to conjure for, though an agreeable relation was established in other ways. It was a disappointment when such servants were outlawed from the air station, probably not long after it was formally taken over by the Navy in the July of 1942. The duties of the askaris of the King's African Rifles were confined to official chores. One might be next to such a putteed but bare-footed figure pushing a Walrus out of the hangar, conscious of his faint acrid smell, not disagreeable, far different from the sewer-like aroma emanating from whites with inadequate bathing facilities. Another phenomenon, early noted, was the sun reflected in scores of tiny points of light from the black (or, more properly, brown) skin of an arm, apt matching of climate and species.

It is not to excuse the inadequacy of my response to East Africa that I emphasize now the conviction I had that, despite the activity in Nairobi, any prolonged stay was out of the question. No doubt, as the months crept by, the feeling grew that to be moved from a cushy, if boring, billet would be grossly unfair, but one was always conscious that the war was ludicrously far from the Kenya Highlands. After a time I did buy a booklet of kitchen Swahili but did not work at it, a complete duffer at languages anyway. When I had discovered and joined the public library in Nairobi I read quite a few books on East Africa which had their due effect on my verse and, later, on *Savage Gold*. I realised there must exist a fringe of educated blacks, probably connected with the university, but I never came across it or enquired about it.

Needless to say, I was intensely sympathetic to the blacks, exploited, as seemed obvious, by both whites and Asians. The colour bar was not so blatant as in South Africa but only because the class of urban blacks, potentially pushy, was comparatively small and feeble. Sometimes I used the Nairobi buses; never took advantage of the rear seats being reserved for 'Europeans'. Such behaviour, not uncommon among servicemen, would be deplored by the white settlers; perhaps did implant in blacks, like the sight of servicemen doing manual jobs, some notion of a more equal order. The big serviceman's canteen in Nairobi, cheap and excellent, was run by Lady Delamere: when three black American G.I.s entered, she bustled up and told them in Swahili they couldn't be served. 'Excuse me, ma'am,' said one, 'I talk no other language but English.' The American presence was fleeting and minute, and caused no other problems that I heard about. Rather odd that one of my first memorable experiences was seeing the all-black band of the K.A.R. playing in the open space in front of the canteen, a selection from Gilbert and Sullivan the first item heard. They were extremely well turned-out, but behind the discipline of their playing could surely be detected some strangeness, as though they might suddenly shift into music with a rhapsodic melody and less metronomic beat, a big-band sound of exciting potential.

Lady Delamere had been the second wife of Lord Delamere, thorn in the flesh of the Colonial Office, able and energetic fighter for the asserted rights of Kenya's white settlers. The tergiversations of East African history, remarkably compressed, will be scarcely known to the ordinary reader of these words, but I have no intention of trying to enlighten, nor am I qualified so to do. White settlement in the Kenya Highlands, a country equatorial but so elevated the climate was non-tropical, had started in the early part of the century, accelerated by restless and jobless officers after the First War. In the Twenties, the place had been a sort of public-school version of the American West, with Asians as the saloon-keepers, undertakers, and other small-part players; blacks as extras; whites as heroes with an admitted sprinkling of villains. The salubrious climate, fertile soil and recent colonization marked it off from British possessions run by the Colonial Service for the benefit, with no serious opposition, of the indigenous population. The whites wanted political power commensurate with the work they were doing and the wealth they were creating.

It was not until 1981 that I read *East African Journey* by Margery Perham, seeing it by chance in the local public library, and thinking it might help with this book, then contemplated. The layers of time involved are, in their nature, fictional; I hope worth separating. Dame Margery's book, though first published in 1976, consists of a journal she kept as an Oxford research fellow in 1923–30, journeying in Kenya and Tanganyika. As I read it, in an epoch when the black republics of Kenya and Tanzania had quite long been established, I was amazedly struck that the scene, the life, she depicted I had arrived at myself a mere dozen years after – that all my memories of Kenya, Uganda and Tanganyika were closer by far to her account of things than to contemporary reality. It would be otiose to provide example of the time shifts and parallels that forcefully arose as I read, but one of them has particular point. In Nairobi, the youthful Margery Perham of 1929–30 went on advice

. . . to the New Stanley Hotel. It was dirty and inefficient and full of white tykes . . . Rowdy groups were always drinking and hanging about the entrance hall . . . As far as I could see Nairobi was largely peopled with young men wearing corduroy plus-fours or shorts, lurid green, orange, blue and purple shirts, and Stetson hats. Some had revolvers in their belts . . . Nairobi . . . is one of the shabbiest and shoddiest towns I have seen in my travels, which is saying a great deal.

By 1942 the New Stanley had been cleaned up and refurbished, perhaps rebuilt, though a few 'white tykes' were still to be seen. Its lounge, convenient of access from the street, was commodious, 'modern' of décor, mirrored walls a feature. Attentive black waiters padded over the parquet floor clad in long white gowns and red fez. I was once reprovingly told by not quite a white tyke but certainly an old boy wearing a green shirt and khaki shorts, a tea-planter from up-country, apropos of tipping, that copper was 'their' currency. But I could never, as did he, bring myself to pass over a single 'Kingi Georgi' for services rendered.

I used the New Stanley quite a lot in the early evening, writing a fair number of lines at one of the many small tables. My usually being alone arose naturally rather than deliberately, though I came to welcome it as the afflatus descended. On the air station we worked tropical routine, starting very early, knocking off at 1 p.m. After lunch everyone 'crashed his swede'. I can scarcely recall being able to sleep at that hour, though not through lack of trying. Constitutional insomnia had already asserted itself, augmented by dyspepsia. Looking back, I see I almost certainly suffered on and off from the peptic ulcers diagnosed some time after the war. Had I reported my symptoms to the M.O. I might in the end have been discharged with a pension – outcome, strange to say, wholly foreign to my character. For though I have often posed as a hypochondriac (once more, the urge to amuse), privately I never regarded myself a weakling. As I often say at seventy, if it weren't for my ailments I should be extremely well. Even at that age I sometimes consider my physique (still identifiable with the athleticism of my schooldays) capable of resuscitation – a rejuvenatory process perhaps reminiscent of the delusions of the heroine of Thomas Mann's *The Black Swan*.

Leaving my colleagues slumbering in the mess hut, I would wander a while through the bleached grass of the Athi Plain, hoping to see game at close quarters, then catch the first 'shore-leave' lorry into Nairobi. Sometimes, eager for the urban life I was used to and loved, I set out for town before that, hoping to bum a lift on the way. The sensations of those walks on the plains comes back: the wakeful yet stupified post-lunch condition only slowly wearing off; the grass, tough yet brittle, impeding the shoes; the palms of the hands somehow stiff – rather a zombie-like progress. One never got far enough into the wild: apt symbolism. Under a sun almost too bright and hot for comfort, the blue hills, backed by rotund white clouds, stayed in the far distance; less far, but seemingly not getting much nearer, were a few brown *rondevaals*, each with its small green *shamba*, and mysterious life unexplored. By a still-moist watercourse a secretary bird might be gravely stalking; once I came on a still-recognizable dead hyena.

In Nairobi I would shop, shop-window gaze, visit the library, until it was a respectable time for the lounge of the New Stanley. Sometimes I wrote my daily letter to Kate beforehand, in the reading room of the *Christian-Science Monitor*: good refuge, but lacking the New Stanley's stimulants. Occasionally, of course, I had to have my hair cut, topic dealt with at what may be considered over-generous length in *Vamp*. I never discovered a satisfactory barber in East Africa, that land of exploration. In the end I patronized an Indian in one of the quieter streets, who was less brutal with scissors and clippers than other Nairobi tonsorial artists, capable of being persuaded to eschew the latter entirely. Notices pertaining to unfamiliar sects, and advertising odd secular events, were exhibited round the mirror, and there must have been additional evidence of a serio-comic life-style we would now dub Naipauline, after that novelist's early fiction about Trinidad. When the hair had been cut one's head was subjected to a brief but tremendously vigorous massage, on the first occasion positively alarming, as though one were being scalped. The memory of this also brings Naipaul to mind; namely, his novel *The Mystic Masseur.*

I drank bottled beer in the New Stanley, rather good, brewed by the East African Brewery Company, but digestively ruinous. Why did I not realise this? Perhaps I did, refused to admit weakness, considered myself still near enough the fit, tough serviceman H.M.S. *Ganges* had made me. But even as an articled clerk I had come to the conclusion beer did not 'suit' me, chose another tipple when I could. After a few beers and rhymes I might well dine alone, usually favouring a tiny restaurant, quite chic for Nairobi but at that still early part of the evening almost deserted. While in the New Stanley, night would have been preparing its swift fall.

> I watch the curious hastened trait of twilight
> Here as I drink my poignant coffee and
> Look out across the wide street through the central
> Island of palms at steady darkening stone.
> Fretted by pale green leaves and silhouettes
> Of banks and consulates, the sky is smooth,
> As smooth as tightened silk, as loose as water . . .

Why I changed this opening of a poem, originally called 'Sadness, Glass, Theory', when preparing my *Collected Poems 1936–1961* is as baffling as Willie's conjuring. As with the other alterations, any improvement now seems minimal: what was lost perhaps most valuable – authentic documentation.

After dinner, on to perhaps one of the two or three cinemas, Indian-owned but usually showing western films, attracting queues and possessing bars, to which many adjourned at the interval, remaining there if the cinematic entertainment was poor, though I was myself prepared to put up with much that was mediocre. By that time I had probably met Bob or Willie by pre-arrangement, more often the former. Asked by the magazine *Poetry (Chicago)* for particulars of my service life for their notes on contributors, I

41

gave some account of these matters, on which they commented that I made darkest Africa sound like Evanston, Illinois.

Presumably a further proximation to provincial America would have been provided had I dilated on the Nairobi society I came to know through Bob, Willie and another classmate in Aberdeen (indeed, in *Ganges*), Tom Duncan, a tall, dark Chartered Accountant, with somewhat of the air of a *boulevardier*, even in the taxi-driver's garb imposed when we were re-rated. These Scots soon established relations with the fellow-countryman who had preceded them, as civilians, to the colony, mainly through the Presbyterian Church – though Tom Duncan's knowing the manager of the East African Breweries may have been extra-ecclesiastical. That friendship led to the four of us spending a weekend at the brewery, dream of every naval rating. Fatal digestive occasion it must have been. The resultant tennis four (I did not play, had scarcely ever played) was surprisingly skilled, Willie's style tinctured by the sleight of hand previously referred to. Willie was also good at badminton, played at the Presbyterian church hall, where I learnt the game, even improved at it. At the church hall I met the Martins, first visiting their house with other servicemen, then quite often going alone.

Stan Martin was manager, perhaps technically works manager, of the flour mill: smallish, slim, gentle; so far as could be seen, of almost saintly character. He, too, suffered from peptic ulcers, farther advanced down that pitted road. He had literary learnings, wrote a one-act comedy-drama, set in a courtroom and played for some charitable purpose in the church hall. The cast included servicemen, among them me, taking me back to schooldays, when I always figured in the school plays, though lacking my brother's flair, revealed by his senile Apothecary described in *Souvenirs*. I may already have mentioned somewhere my foolishly playing Phoebe, the maid at Dotheboys Hall, 'straight' (in a dramatization from *Nicholas Nickleby*), and I believe as an actor I never properly 'let myself go', unless to a degree as Flute in the Boarders' Concert production of the last act of the *Dream*, more notable for Gorill's Hypolita, touched on in *Souvenirs*.

The single performance of Stan Martin's play may have been the origin of a nightmarish dream, still recurring: I am about to step on the boards and I do not know my lines. In the actuality I had the script out of sight below the top of the jury-box and with judicious squinting and some ad-libbing got through the ordeal pretty well. Why did I not learn my part? Fundamental haziness of memory was partly to blame, but I expect I subconsciously thought the whole enterprise *infra dig*. Some deeper significance may inhere. I played the part, a juror putting in his oar more than somewhat, as an elderly blimpish ex-military man, escaping from the restrained Phoebe tradition by a spell beforehand in the New Stanley. Little did I reck that forty years on I should be accused of putting over this character in real life.

Stan once showed me round the flour mill. I was struck by its vertical production line, powered by gravity. There was also mechanical power, of course, and one day Stan came home and said he had had to deal with a black whose arm had been caught in the belting and torn off. How I admired his ability, housed in such a seemingly frail shell, to deal with the appalling! – calling in question my own squeamishness, and continuing luck with the real business of the war. In my collection of poems, mainly about Africa, *A Lost Season*, some of the strongest feeling is reserved for mere news about the war, in a piece called 'October 1942'. When I came to revise it for the *Collected Poems* of 1962 I was going to retitle it 'The Defence of Stalingrad', then thought that too pretentious, and simply generalised it a little as 'Autumn 1942'. Surely the events of the Stalingrad battle, and the subsequent reading of Alexander Werth's remarkable book *The Year of Stalingrad* (1946), prolonged my sympathy for the Soviet Union during the early post-war years.

Stan must have been in his mid-forties, his wife Hilda a few years younger. As I write this she is still alive, still in Kenya, where she stuck it out through all that followed after the war, gaining an M.B.E. for her work in Government service. At the time I speak of, however, she was secretary to the editor of the *East African Standard*: typical of her vigour and enterprise that she arranged for the paper to report my presence in the colony and print in two issues, in well-displayed boxes, poems from *The Middle of a War*. The couple had only one child, a daughter of eighteen, who had inherited her father's character. Strange for a complete outsider temporarily to step into the lives of others and observe the state of play without himself quite becoming involved – a feature of existence that fiction often ignores or exaggerates.

The Martins' hospitality extended to a good many servicemen, but I believe I was specially privileged in their friendship. The ambience offered was similar to that I had been brought up in – utterly unstrained, modest, and informal comfort. It is a mark of the ease of our relations that agreeable trivialities now come to mind – Hilda putting it on the menu when I casually said I liked cold rice pudding; Hazel running me in their car to the lower camp entrance late at night; messing about with a longish poem called 'Teba' in their sitting-room, alone in the house save for the 'houseboy', for an hour or so part of ordinary life once more.

If by some stretch of imagination there could be said to be a white proletariat in Nairobi, it consisted of employees of the railway, I think a quite numerous class, who had their own club. It seems unlikely that honorary membership of the club had been conferred on all servicemen stationed in Nairobi, but that was the status enjoyed by Willie, Bob, Tom and myself. Some Hibernian wangling must have been involved, myself a Sassenach beneficiary. I do not recall much social intercourse on my part with the club members, only playing snooker there late in the evenings, a black steward available to bring beer and perform other chores, the members boozing distantly in the bars. A working-man's club with large knobs on may be envisaged.

4. Green, Black, Brown

Finally, preferences of a more profound and more disinterested kind diversify the memories of different people, so that a poet, for example, who has almost entirely forgotten certain facts which someone else is able to recall will, nevertheless, have retained – what for him is more important – a fleeting impression.

– Proust: *Time Regained*, trans. Andreas Mayor

Whether, before the new draft arrived and assumed virtual power in the 'Special W/T Section', the clique ever went hunting in the car previously mentioned is lost to history. If the vehicle were not successfully rehabilitated I do not know why they did not use the section's van, for a strict regard for legality in that area seems unlikely. The van was often officially and unofficially driven by a Leading Air Fitter in the electrical branch, yet another Scot, rather good-looking, a genuine tradesman who had worked for British Thompson Houston. I had from Blair a couple of extra-curricular driving lessons, for though my mother owned a car in my latter days at home I never drove it, perhaps still suffused with a D. H. Lawrentian sense of the motor-car being impossibly bourgeois and anti-life. I have a clear mental picture of steering the van along the road from the camp across the plain, and seeing, with increasing anxiety, against the background of the Ngong Hills, another vehicle approaching. Would I miss it? The road was strait.

Blair one afternoon took me and a few others for a spin a little way into those hills. It was really my first venture away from what might be called Africa's beaten tracks. I had written a couple of rather formal poems with Africa as background ('Parabolas of grief, the hills' sort of affair) but suddenly, returning from the Ngong outing, a way to fulfil the wish to write about the country was revealed. It was the business over again of finding myself able to write about service life.

> Can you be much surprised at what the hills
> Contain? The girls run up the slope,
> Their oiled and shaven heads like caramels.
> Behind them is the village, its corrugated
> Iron and, like a wicked habit, the store.
> The villagers cough, the sacking blows from the naked
> Skin of a child, a white scum on his lips.
> The youths come down in feathers from the summit.
> And over them all a gigantic frescoed sky.
>
> (from 'The Green Hills of Africa', original version)

This is what was seen on the brief van trip. It may be thought to be laying it on a bit to imply that such simple and direct verse needed some sort of prior revelation. Moreover, the actual poetic achievement probably seems slight today. But however modest the shift in these matters, some not easily achieved, often unwilled augmentation of power must usually be found by the poet. I wrote a few descriptive pieces of 'The Green Hills of Africa' kind, comparatively unclogged by the lingering ideology of the Thirties (though as can be seen from line five of the foregoing extract, there was still a touch of what we thought of then as 'later' Auden). The landscape of East Africa, let alone its people and fauna, makes a deep impression on travellers. The general effect could scarcely be put better than in Margery Perham's diary:

> The land here lies in fold after fold, each one long, low and smooth but rising here and there where a layer of granite has ridged itself against the erosion of wind and water. The granite has been split into fragments by the action of day and night, of heat and cold, and now each summit is a tumbled mass of grey stone, tufted with harsh vegetation, spiked and bladed stuff, and the refuge of lions, leopards and hyenas. These crested folds could be seen from where I was walking (three-quarter's up one of them), stretching to a distance seldom seen – I surmise – in other continents except on a clear day, from mountains. There seemed no end to these folds. It was as though they did not

disappear in the haze but rather as though your eyes could not see any further out over that blue sequence. The light spotting of shrub and thorn gives the blueness.

My reading in East African history and anthropology gave some subsequent poems an extra dimension. Bringing in the war and the question of profound social change was perhaps less successful, though to a few such pieces some contemporary readers responded with sympathy.

> . . . some great faculty
> Like hands, has been eternally lost and all
> Our virtues now are the high and horrible
> Ones of a streaming wound which heals in evil.

I quote from the Stalingrad poem, mentioned already. Though the outcome of the battle, great hinge of the war, was a sensational German downfall, the news of it, of the sufferings of its participants, came in agonizing instalments, and the poem's last two stanzas do, I see now, to some degree embody a pessimistic yearning about humanity which was renewed and intensified – and persisted – after the atom bombs had been dropped on Japan. I might add, bathetically, that for the 1962 *Collected Poems* I did not alter the end of the poem at all; sensible decision. In general, the revisions I made to *A Lost Season* removed some slapdashery but whether I effected many real improvements I would now think doubtful. What the poems needed was more work on them in the New Stanley lounge and other haunts of the Muse.

Most of the African poems appeared in John Lehmann's *New Writing*, in both its Penguin and hardback forms, Kate acting as typist and literary agent, for anthologies and other periodicals were also involved. The second impression of *The Middle of a War* and the phenomenal circulation of *Penguin New Writing* must have peaked such fame as I've enjoyed to a height not reached thereafter. This had no effect I can recall on my style and output. What did count was John Lehmann's critical support, the constant sense that the best of my work would find its way into print in an ambience of which I wholly approved. As already implied, John's deep desire was to find and encourage writing that would reflect the scale and intensity of the world conflict. Yet being a man of the Thirties he required such writing to be underpinned by observation, by fact.

47

Mere rhetoric was unlikely to get past him. All that was very useful to me. I wonder what he would have said if I had anticipated a side of my verse that showed a few decades later, and dealt ironically with the trivialities of existence. Almost certainly shaking his head a little, he would have chosen the best of that, too, for his romantic nature was balanced by a love of Byron's comic poetry (and his father had, of course, been a notable writer of light verse).

I had rather thought that being a C.W. candidate at H.M.S. *Ganges* had marked me for an eventual commission even though I had deviated from the executive branch into radar – acquisition of the status, like beatification, inevitably postponed by investigative bureaucracy; that process even more prolonged in such a new technical field. However, looking at the fragmentary journal, I see that in September 1942 I was called out of the iffy hut by one of the officers from the new draft and asked, as though introducing a fresh theme, if I had ever thought about a commission. The following month I was actually set a written test, disconcertingly on wireless telegraphy and general electrics, not thought of since that prelimi- nary course in Aberdeen. It seems I did well; had then to give personal details for completion of the form necessary to activate once more the mysterious C.W. machinery. I say in the journal I only allowed the recommendation to go forward to gain the chance of returning prematurely to the U.K., a statement I see no reason to doubt. Certainly the *animus revetendi* (as the phrase used to go, doing private international law in student days) was intense.

The officer responsible (or jointly so) for this touch on my destiny's tiller possessed the Wodehousian (or, more accurately, early Waughian) name of Peter Lavender, living up to it with somewhat of the voice and manner of a musical-comedy juvenile lead, more likely the second lead, being smallish and humorous rather than tallish and romantic. I expect some Admiralty Fleet Order or other *ukase* had laid on him the duty of sniffing out potential radar officers, but elements existed of a fellow feeling between us, restricted though our contacts were. The journal notes barely that my position in the section had subtly changed, that I was becoming 'a sort of personage'. Though the *Vamp Till Ready* syndrome was still largely operant, I was, after all, thirty years old and had been established in a quite decent civilian post. But how the 'personage' propagated its qualities memory fails to recall (though no effort of will would be involved), except that towards the end of the year I was asked to help with the defence of a rating on some homosexual charge. Probably Peter Lavender's completion of the C.W. form had apprised him of my profession, and he had gossiped in the wardroom, as schoolmasters gossip in the common-room about their pupils. I worked on the submission on behalf of the accused by his 'next friend', and did some research in a manual of military law. I expect I missed the talents in this line of Richard Flower, described in *Vamp*, though the result was as good as could be expected. The business brought me into direct contact with the station's head of supply branch, a Commander (S) of imposing build and floridity, called, appropriately, Rump (though somewhat disappointingly spelt, as I discovered during the case, Rumph). It is typical of life – my life, at least – that much later some information came to me about Commander Rumph's existence in Nairobi, curious, but too vague in my mind now to set down.

How incompletely one appreciated in youth – still does, to some extent – one's effect on others! I remember – the thing out of mind for forty years – that setting out on foot for Nairobi I was once picked up by the station commander in a little open sports car. We chatted, perhaps touched on former days: may have been he who eventually brought the homosexual client. He was in natty khaki, probably off to his exalted version of a 'baron'. I sometimes saw him with self-evident big-wigs in the best seats at the concerts and other entertainments in Nairobi's theatre. But the chic car and the petrol to run it were the most striking symbols of his status in the society among which, like me, he had so unexpectedly and fleetingly descended. To acquire them, how much string- pulling and throwing about of weight was required? Through diffidence, guilt, considera-tion for others, and a few other disabling traits, I never did enough of that sort of thing during my later career; only as a Governor of the B.B.C. willy-nilly getting some tit-bits put on my plate.

The concerts I remember were given by a fine fiddler and pianist, the latter none other than Ivor Keys, later Professor of Music at Birmingham University, whose excellent monograph on Brahms's chamber music happens to lie on one of my loudspeakers as I write. In 1942 he was in the Army, stationed in or near Nairobi, a slim, fair twenty-three year old. I used to speculate about the divinatory or driving powers of his parents, who anticipatorily had had him christened thus: indeed, wondering if the name might not be an apt pseudonym adopted for the 'showbiz' side of his life, like the tall music-hall comedienne, a favourite of my mother's, Lily Long. However, this latter notion could scarcely be maintained, for no flicker of the least frivolity, in manner or repertoire, disturbed the recitals – which included the Brahms sonatas and much Beethoven (a performance of the latter's op. 96 in G remembered to this day). The duo, as had the Durban Symphony Orchestra, provided an amazing glimpse of the desired life of art which one might return to or, more accurately, come to embrace with more fervour and devotion than heretofore.

At the theatre the local amateur operatic society gave a performance of Gounod's *Faust*. I went with the Martins: whether I should have gone under my own steam is extremely doubtful, at that epoch scorning composers like Gounod (though I knew every note of the ballet music, relic of pier-end days). When the preliminaries (vamp till ready music of supreme effectiveness) to the bass aria 'Veau d'or' started up I must have thought of Stanley Birch, one of the 'two pianists' at school, for this was an example he educed of great melodies. I could have hummed the initial twiddly bits and launched into the piece itself, so thoroughly had Birch imprinted it on my adolescent memory. What is surprisingly open now is whether the opera was done in costume or as a concert version. Given the presumed scarcity of tights and cloaks and so forth in Central Africa in 1942, one inclines to the latter, in which case the memorable episode of the soprano's underwear may well have occurred during one of Gretchen's arias and not at a concert of individual items.

The singer concerned was a personable local young woman with a good voice. One immediately noticed her carelessness in entering with an inch of white slip showing below her green dress. As the song progressed the whiteness slowly came down, eventually revealing itself as the comparatively voluminous garment called French Knickers. For me, hilarity was checked by embarrassment; would have been so even without the presence beside me of the Martin ladies. The soprano courageously continued, chance, or possibly muscular control, bringing the final descent to her feet only at the end of the song, when she stepped out of the crumpled knickers, picked them up, and walked off the stage to applause quite sensational in its warmth. One could not help speculating, when she returned, whether the garment had been restored, the question, if the occasion was indeed *Faust*, having rather more than mere prurient undertones.

In such ways the time wore on. To my surprise (the lenitive scarcely seeming part of service abroad) entitlement to leave arose. Whether a railway warrant came with the entitlement, so to speak,

I do not know, but in any event Willie Robertson conceived a grandiose plan for the leave we agreed to take together. Perhaps through contacts at the Railway Club, he procured for us an interview with the Passenger Traffic Superintendent (or title to that effect) of the East African railway (a Scot, it need hardly be said), and put to him the proposition that we should have warrants to Kampala, Uganda, returning to Nairobi via Lake Victoria – the detour itself involving goodness knows how many hundred miles, and aboard a company steamer. Associating myself with this request seemed as outrageous as holding the hat while Gilbert Waller sang in the street, youthful episode familiar to readers of my earlier memoirs. But Willie conducted the interview with his inimitable blend of the feelingly serious and the jocular, bringing in common Hibernian memories, and drawing on the know-how acquired behind the public counter of the shipping line he had served in civvy street. The outcome was that the Superintendent agreed to honour the warrants, with the reasonable proviso that meals on the steamers were not included. He must surely have also provided some chit so as to ensure our warrants being filled in with the amazing route adumbrated – for I see now the responsible character in the R.P.O.'s office like one of the barrack stanchions in Alan Ross' poem of that title:

> their complexions, like rinds
> Of bacon, and on their fingers the ring
> Like a knuckleduster that chased the scrawl
> Of their antique penmanship . . .

So I set off on the most considerable unforced journey of my life; a journey I could only recapture, if then, by reading and trying to embroider the letters I wrote to Kate, which I do not intend to do. I know they would be too frail a foundation for anything other than the insubstantial. The makings of a chapter were there at the time, but apart from the letters, essentially perfunctory if sincere and nostalgic, I made no record. That deficiency seems the more venal because of my African reading, and the eagerness with which I looked out of the train for the potash lakes of the Kenya Highlands, for example, and the Nile pouring out of the lake's plug-hole at Jinja. There were no poems, either, and the uneasy question arises for a writer how much experience loses if not assimilated in a literary way.

51

We had a night or two at Kampala before catching the lake steamer at Entebbe, Kampala's port, staying at the town's premier hotel, the Imperial, quite luxurious. Willie must have had some baronial introduction, for he took a photograph of me by a swimming pool (probably attached to a club) sitting next to a fellow resembling Alfred Hitchcock who has nevertheless fallen completely from memory. It may have been he who gave me a snapshot of the giant crocodile Lutembe emerging from lake reeds, for this was not taken by Willie: we were driven to the spot, called 'Lutembe, Lutembe', as instructed, but the beast failed to respond (unlike Fafner on being similarly called in Act II of *Siegfried*), whether to our disappointment or relief, who knows? Though not extensive at that date, the shops and boulevards of Kampala were attractive to two townees; moreover, Ugandan society was immediately detectable as superior to Kenyan. Absent, the powerful, exploitive, but disgruntled class of white settlers, baronial in a Shakespearean sense: one felt the country was being run entirely for the benefit of the indigenous population – in Kampala, black, tall and stately, the women headgeared and swathed in bright cloth (carrying off even the banal designs of Lancashire mills), a dramatic change from the scurrying brown Kikuyu women of Nairobi and its environs, shaven heads often bent against a strap bearing some back-breaking load. How awful that, as I write, independent Uganda has lapsed into tribal anarchy and atrocities just as bad, one guesses, as before the British arrived. Who could have prognosticated that as the outcome of a further forty years of history?

The lake steamer may be envisaged as resembling the German gunboat more than Humphrey Bogart's *African Queen*, in the eponymous film. It was of substantial Scottish workmanship, greatly pleasing to Willie. The ship's officers were almost equally Scottish: Willie was soon on terms, discovering friends, ancestors and tramroutes in common, in Hibernian fashion. Stepping aboard in the early morning at steamy Entebbe, the quay piled with cargo, in bustling and tuneful process of being loaded by native labour, one suddenly felt part of a Conradian routine, commonplace but fated. Willie and I were carrying not kitbags but the green canvas suitcases available from pusser's stores. One says that, but the Nairobi store had been *non est* or at any rate ill-stocked until recent times, when queuing for its sudden bounties had not unpleasantly passed the best part of a morning. In my case, acquisition of a suitcase had accompanied that of a raincoat (the very raincoat subsequently transmogrified into an officer's garment, as sufficiently described in *Vamp*), and a safety razor that lasted even longer into post-war civilian life, its exotic brand-name *Ruby Ring*, confirmed by a red band near the base of the handle. (But re-writing these pages, it comes to me that albeit the razor's red feature is indubitable – though in fact fairly quickly being eroded through use – 'Ruby Ring' was actually the name of a pre-war brand of silk, or artificial silk, women's stocking; the red band being seen or encountered where the silk changed to lisle, the latter more apt to withstand the depredations of the rubber and metal suspender attachment. If so, the excellent razor's name is unfortunately among the forgotten).

Wandering round Kampala had included the perennial search for reading matter. But what did I peruse during those hours on deck? Perhaps one day still, a book idly opened will bring back the steamer throbbing through the calm, sometimes out of sight of land in the amazing lake that could sink Wales. The motion made the equatorial sun deceptive. By the time we put in at Masaka, Willie's thighs, where his shorts had ridden up, had been painfully burned, his fair skin reddening, never bronzing. We walked down the main, perhaps only, street, a small collection of godowns run by Asiatic shopkeepers, Willie in search of a sun-burn remedy. A fair range of toilet articles was available – combs, scissors, brilliantine – even, it occurs to me, that hair-dressing popular at my school, Seafolde House, *Anzora Viola*, the name in the context taking on a colonial character, as of some former Spanish or Portuguese possession. Hanging cards of powders and phials indicated the pill-peddling assiduity of some African equivalent of Bobby (the manufacturing chemists' commercial traveller who had vainly loved me in my youth, and through whom, as *Souvenirs* tells, had indirectly come the revelation of the Auden school of poets). But since the clientèle in Masaka lacked pale complexions, a specific for Willie's discomfort was not to be found. His tall, raw-boned, sandyish wavy-haired presence, though not now bearded, was given a zombie touch by the white-rimmed sunglasses he often affected, and would not in any event have gone unnoticed: as it was, pretty general interest was roused in his problem, eventually attacked in characteristic Indian fashion by one of the shopkeepers. Unable to bear the absence of business or knowledge of therapy, he confidently recommended the application of *ghee*, the culinary clarified butter which in my experience has never seemed other than rancid, like the butter improbably devoured by the cat in T. S. Eliot's poem. So Willie

53

was duly anointed, whether being sold a supply of *ghee* for future application I do not recollect. What does come back is that his thighs became a target for the numerous Masaka flies.

As on the *Capetown Castle*, companionship with Willie on this journey was utterly harmonious. In *The Perfect Fool* I work in an example or two of the fictional Willie's set-piece jokes. The real Willie's fund of them seemed perpetually renewed, even in Central Africa. A boring bar raconteur is not to be envisaged: his stories were an extension of his own humour, and always succinctly told, singly, and at intervals. They were usually improper, but offensiveness was removed by his own essentially innocent and domesticated character. Some may have been invented by him, for occasionally they pursued a theme over a few days. A woman goes into a bow-legged chemist's. 'Have you got camphor balls?' 'No, madam. I always walk like this.' Later, a woman (perhaps the same woman) goes into a department store and asks a bow-legged shop-walker: 'Where can I get talcum powder?' 'Walk this way, madam.' 'If I walked that way I wouldn't need talcum powder.' How strange now seem the period touches in such things! Bow-legs, in the Glasgow of Willie's youth and the Oldham of mine, were a commonplace, legacy of ricketts. Indeed, a favourite joke of mine when a boy concerned a bow-legged man being measured for a pair of trousers. The tailor is fussing inordinately with his tape measure until the customer (plainly an Oldhamer) says exasperatedly: 'Thee just mak' 'um straight. A'll bend 'um.'

The food we had to pay for on board was completely unmemorable. The passengers ate in the stateroom with such officers as were off watch. The former were few in number, changing at every port; mostly, it seems to me now, missionaries. The most attractive place called at was Bukoba: a small bay of pale sand we strolled along, the steamer sending up smoke at the jetty at one end. There was time to bathe, which I did, forgetting until afterwards Lutembe's champing tribe. Late in the afternoon a white-habited monk arrived on a motor-cycle and sidecar for supplies from the ship, a Greeneish touch to the Conradian picture. Musoma, in what was then Tanganyika, seemed the most African of the ports. In the market there, Willie with his box Brownie snapped an attractive young girl, bare-breasted, holding a load on her neat head; and an old witch-woman with brass headgear and loaded with charms. Some slight coin passed from Willie on each of these occasions, to the astonishment of the girl, who had to be encouraged by the bystanders to accept it: the witch was blasé – indeed, conceivably got herself up specially for steamer-call days, and chasséd about a bit when the camera was pointed at her. For the literary parallel vis-à-vis the indigenous life, one would have had to go back to the Elizabethans.

I turn once more to Margery Perham's journal-letters (again, so vivid and succinct) for a description of an experience similar to one of ours in this southern part of the lake, not uncharacteristic of the astounding exaggerations of Central Africa:

> We caught the boat at 7.30 in the morning back to Mwanza and spent all day on board, getting in at 6 o'clock. I don't think I have said anything about the lake-fly. It is the curse of this side of the lake coast. It is bred out of the water, a minute spot of a creature, and it comes up like smoke and blows ashore in the wind . . . A cloud of the fly hit our ship and the result was misery. Where you sit down your frock is marked by innumerable spots of squashed fly. They smothered the food and the lights. The captain told me he once found a canoe with four natives all dead. Their mouths, noses, ears and eyes full of fly. A 'spout' of them must have arisen just under the boat.

We disembarked at Kisumu, back in Kenya, whence we were to return by train to Nairobi: Willie had an introduction to a couple there whose name and very physical presences escape me – unforgivably so, for I stayed with them when Willie went on to Nairobi without me, on some further baronial engagement. But perhaps the Kisumu barons were merely hotel-keepers and I duly paid for my accommodation. One of only two surviving Kisumu memories tends to confirm this: seeing from an overlooking room a wild funeral procession along the main street. The other is of spending half a day with an elderly Kisumu solicitor, which included going with him when he appeared before the Registrar of the Court in chambers. I was astonished when fags were offered round by the solicitor and we all lit up before the application, or whatever it was, was made, and smoked through the proceedings. In the solicitor's office the managing clerk was a grave Parsee in frock-coat and light trousers, seemingly the type of responsible subordinate I much relied on in the Woolwich Solicitor's Department. The solicitor, whom I took to, said he was in sore need of a younger partner: why didn't I get in touch with him when the war was over? He was quite serious, even mentioned some attractive share of the profits: prospects were good, the Asians were so litigious. Though I saw clearly that Kenya's racial problems were insoluble in any rational way, I gave the proposition fleeting consideration. What a queer turn to life it would have been, perhaps leading down some popular fictional road; Somerset Maugham Avenue, say.

It was for an odd day or two, at the end of this leave, that I must have stayed with the Martins: the occasion of working on 'Teba' previously mentioned. 'Working' one says (the ambitious word, as applied to literary activity rather than a bread and butter job, I heard first from Julian Symons in the late Thirties, and have only used it myself in that context in comparatively recent years, and then with self-amused unease – 'playing' the participle seemingly more appropriate), though my recollection is of merely copying out the first draft, with such corrections and improvements as would come out in the wash. The poem is about the collision of tribal and urban African society, rather more than 200 lines. When I came to look at it for inclusion in my *Collected Poems* of 1962 I was especially mortified by its clumsiness.

> It was a single warrior sent
> By the tribe's chief to its erring member,
> So feminine and insolent
> In look, his voice so deep in timbre,
> With a spear which made Teba remember
> The slightly archaic past, the whole
> Ritual in which he had a role.

Probably I have already said enough about re-writing these African poems, but 'Teba' presented an extra problem of being encased in the hard shell of an ababbcc stanza form, and I was conscious even in 1962 of its being more justly written off than re-written. But my thriftiness in life has extended to poems. The foregoing stanza was one whose deficiencies I must have felt could not be reprinted, the illegitimate rhyme 'member'/'remember' probably the most vexing. I suppose, too, 'slightly archaic' seemed an impression of prose rather than an illumination of poetry. This is how I revised the stanza: some pedagogic corrections, undoubtedly, but overall improvement, *quaere*:

> A warrior that the chief had sent,
> The many's message to the one,

So feminine and insolent
In look, his voice so deep in tone,
Whose trappings wakened Teba's own
Archaic past, the ritual
In which he once had played a role.

A little while ago, I had occasion to remind John Grigg, the historian, a present neighbour in Blackheath, of my African poems. I myself had been reminded by Margery Perham's book that his father, as Sir Edward Grigg, had been Governor-General of Kenya, and it turned out that John had passed part of his infancy there. He read or re-read the poems, singling out 'Teba' with unprompted generosity. I record this not to commend the piece but to indicate the mysterious life and death of literary work, part of it sometimes in a mere catatonic trance, capable of resuscitation by a prince's chance arrival. Needless to say, the outrageous coincidences of life connect me further with the Griggs: in my grandfather's day Edward Grigg was Conservative M.P. for Oldham, my grandfather a pillar of the local party; the youthful John Grigg left with impressions of Oldham analogous to those of Kenya (becoming more familiar with its bizarreries, no doubt, during the Fifties, when he contested one of its Parliamentary constituencies).

Part of the deal offered by the Navy to those embarking on the career of radar mechanic was promotion to leading hand at the end of the course (so derided by the Petty Officer of the clique), and then promotion to Petty Officer a year after that. Would the latter promise be fulfilled; the ponderous machine of the Andrew engage with its remote cogs in Nairobi? There was a good deal of anxiety among those sweating on the top line for this amelioration in pay and conditions, an attendant and almost comparable worry being the securing of the necessary physical indications of higher rank should the promotion come through. In the event, the necessary signal arrived on the dot – signals, rather; for promotion for Willie and me was a week after the others on account of our having had to re-sit the practical test at the end of the Lee-on-the-Solent course, as related in *Vamp*. What an emotional week it must have been for us seeing Tom Duncan *et al* ascend to a higher sphere! But all came right in the end. Moreover, Blair (who had been sweating on *his* promotion in the electrical branch), with a generosity that still staggers me, gave me a precious Petty Officer's cap-badge, with gold wire, image of a girl's hair in an Elizabethan love poem, at

57

that time unobtainable in pusser's stores. Thus was immediately satisfied the near-mystical need felt in the Services for appearance to correspond to status (and which later I was to observe at the Admiralty in the almost miraculously simultaneous-with-promotion transformation of three stripes to four, even two to two-and-a-half). As a matter of fact, since one had only acting rank until confirmation after a further year, one was strictly not entitled until then to wear a P.O.'s cap badge, merely the crossed hooks on the sleeve.

A small subscription was paid for membership of the P.O.s' mess but the comestible additions thereby facilitated seemed insignificant, mainly the provision of bottles of sauce and pickles for the table. In the bar, however, spirits were not infrequently available: some Australian gin arrived, the brand-name of which I remembered for many years, that gave me a two-day hangover. And there were comfortable chairs. It was strange – Madam Verdurin among the aristos, almost – hobnobbing with those who, the very day before promotion, had been set in positions of authority, even control over one's destiny, like the R.P.O. Did one knock back Australian gin lolling next to the P.O. of the clique, or had he by then voyaged to India with Lieutenant Fagg?

As with all promotion, there came a sense that the new status was not quite what it had been when longed for from afar, not least because shared with some fellow-promotees less worthy in one's own eyes than oneself. Non-technical duties were light: I was faintly apprehensive when my turn came to be P.O. for the day, but all I remember of that is going round at night with the (black) sergeant of the K.A.R. to inspect the guard posts, which were manned by *askaris*. The experience formed the basis of a poem, 'The White Conscript and the Black Conscript', which puts the issues of colonialism, war, multi-racial society, in terms which today seem astonishingly simple, if not simplistic, yet which I would not wish to disown:

> If only I could tell you
> That in my country there
> Are millions as poor as you
> And almost as unfree: if I could share
> Our burdens of despair!

By then I knew a little about the Kenyan tribes, and had been to a remarkable display of tribal dancing at Nairobi's football stadium (or perhaps some entirely different venue, for don't I remember dust rising through the car headlights illuminating the dancers?). So at the guard posts I essayed a bit of chat with the *askaris*, my scullery Swahili barely augmented by the sergeant's similar English; the tribal languages must also have been a barrier. Nevertheless, some communication occurred, as the poem indicates, not least astonishment that I should be able to utter the names of tribes. Moreover, there was a bit of illegal cigarette smoking and the general agreement, previously touched on, about the comic nature of minute to minute existence.

5.   Petty Officer's Mess

Sir Dysentry Malaria,
A famous brigadier,
Commands the whole sub-area . . .

– Roy Campbell

I could not have been a petty officer for very long when it was
arranged I should go to R.N.A.S., Tanga, to lecture to aircrews
about I.F.F. The term set was a month, but one had gloomy
forebodings that once plucked from the cushy number at Nairobi
one would never return. Tanga was on the Tanganyikan coast,
somewhat north of Zanzibar. In early April 1943 I went by train
to Mombasa, by Naval truck to nearby Port Reitz, and then by air
to the naval air station at Tanga. In the outer world the Tunisian
invasion would be proceeding, no substitute for the Second Front,
though who was I to think it tame? Even after the marvellous
triumph of Stalingrad, there would be a sense of unease about the
Russian ability to withstand another German summer offensive.
One was just as much at the mercy of the news as a civilian.

At that epoch air travel was by no means the commonplace it
became soon after the war. For me, apprehensive of heights, it was
only to be borne in the line of duty, like climbing the mast at
H.M.S. *Ganges*, as adumbrated in *Vamp*. As a matter of fact I had
already been in the air. I went up in a (bombless) Blenheim bomber
from the R.A.F. station at Nairobi just to see (or, rather, hear –
for the response could be monitored through earphones, the pulse-
rate having an audio frequency) how the I.F.F. set behaved in
action. The Blenheim homed on a beacon (perhaps the ASV test

60

apparatus, but my grasp of technicalities at this distance of time is shaky) set up outside the Special W/T hanger. I also had the opportunity to see the working of the Blenheim's ASV set. One or the other set was in the bubble in the forward belly of the aircraft (the Observer's position) so a certain amount of crawling about in mid-flight was entailed, perhaps the best analogy being the making of a propaganda film illustrative of heroism in the air. Even the staggering sight of the snows of both Kilimanjaro and Mount Kenya, pimple and carnivore's tooth respectively, rising out of the brownish haze, did not alleviate the pretty constant sense of unease, peaking as we banked and dropped down air-pockets – motions all too reminiscent of the Velvet Coaster, on Blackpool's Pleasure Beach, which as a boy I tried to dissuade adults from taking me on. (Later, an even more fearful ride, the Big Dipper, usurped its place, but by then I was old enough to be firm, though still shame-faced, about saying no). My respect for authority on most occasions (undoubtedly allied to timidity) was shown on the pilot's initial appearance in helmet and neutral overalls by my addressing him as 'sir', only later realising he must have been a mere sergeant-pilot, and remorsefully kicking myself. Quite typical of the radar of those days, possibly of all war's apparatus, that so far as I could tell the I.F.F. set was not being triggered; inconclusiveness undissipated by Bob Park, on duty at the beacon, when I returned to the womb of the iffy hut.

At Port Reitz the transporting aircraft proved to be an Albacore, biplane similar to the Swordfish, but enclosing the occupants instead of leaving their busts in the open air. In the early days of the clique I had bostiked the aerial bollards of many an Albacore, skinned my knuckles removing for repair its devilishly situated ASV units. I was not reassured by finding the passenger (normally observer) section rusty, and swimming in tropical rainwater. I shared the flight with a naval medical officer, though not the one quite soon to become a familiar figure. We were airborne for a mere half hour, the element not greatly alarming at this second essay; some emotion to spare for the sight of the green island shapes in the bluest of seas as we flew south down the coast. I got to R.N.A.S., Tanga, a mere clearing in the palm trees, in the null part of the afternoon. The administrative hut was like the sheriff's office in an old western movie. My arrival had not been signalled, or the signal lost. Some duty messenger was raised to convey me to the Chief Petty Officer's Mess, where the Master-at-Arms (who alone, apparently, could

61

receive me) was still enjoying his siesta. The heat was intense, far different from Nairobi's galvanizing sunshine and rare air.

I have already, more than once, touched on the question of khaki, incongruous colour, it seemed at first, vis-à-vis the navy. Though in Nairobi I started by going ashore in whites, when it became apparent that an acceptable rig was khaki shirt, and long khaki trousers (shorts in the evenings were banned on account of mosquitos), I adopted it, like many others, as more practical. I had a pair of longs, perhaps two, made at an Indian tailor's. I also got him to make a khaki cap-cover for my taxi-driver's cap. Typical of Indian thrift, even more extreme than my own, that when I came to what should have been the happy moment of putting cap-cover on cap I found it had been tailored too exiguously to fit. Whether I took it back or went elsewhere or simply continued to wear the regulation white cap-cover is a dim botheration in which readers may well not feel deeply engaged. The khaki shirts issued at Lee were no more than fairly adequate working shirts, hardly consonant with even an Indian-tailored pair of longs. In the window of a Nairobi men's outfitters I saw a khaki shirt that appealed to me: flannel, dark of hue, expensive. I pondered the textile side of the question, deciding in the end that flannel, though lacking coolness, had the virtue of absorbing sweat. As to cost, I reminded myself the dear old Woolwich was still making up my salary (the burden on its funds somewhat diminished after I had been promoted Petty Officer).

Entering the C.P.O.'s mess at Tanga, cap (whatever colour of cap-cover) politely under my arm, the foregoing shirt was the one I was wearing. Its charisma is the only way I can account for the Master-at-Arms (I let for the moment the term stand without ambiguity) addressing me at once as 'sir' when I enquired where I was to go. The Blenheim pilot business was bouleversed. I was profoundly embarrassed, realising I had long weeks, perhaps months, to live with his damaged *amour propre*. No use my respectfully adding 'Chief' to every phrase, for that was exactly what a conscientious officer would do. The misunderstanding was soon cleared up, perhaps by my producing a draft chit if such was in my possession; quite likely, I being the draft's sole member. A further question arises, not at all resolved by use of 'Chief' rather than 'Master-at-Arms', for the titles were interchangeable in common parlance, certainly in the slacker Fleet Air Arm. Was the individual to whom I spoke on that initiatory occasion, lounging with a few other 'Chiefs' in an ambience far different from the chic

Chiefs' Mess of H.M.S. *Mermaid* (as sketched in *Vamp*), actually the 'jaunty', the Master-at-Arms, whose reputed persona and habits I quickly became aware of? It may be said that in such a relatively small community I must have known, should have remembered; but the *vrai* Jaunty, like many legendary characters, was blurred in reality and has become even less real with the passing of time.

I was assigned to a hut among the palms. It was not far from the P.O.s' Mess, some of the features of which appear in my eponymous poem, notably the pet monkeys, emblem in the poem for the human condition; reminiscent of the Lieutenant-Commander's hobby at Seafield Park (mentioned in *Vamp*), perhaps some archetypal naval preoccupation.

> The monkeys near the mess (where we all eat
> And dream) I saw tonight select with neat
> And brittle fingers dirty scraps, and fight,
> And then look pensive in the fading light,
>   And after pick their feet.
>
> They are secured by straps about their slender
> Waists, and the straps to chains. Most sad and tender,
> They clasp each other and look round with eyes
> Like ours at what their strange captivities
>   Invisibly engender.

Mosquito nets I seem to think were optional in Nairobi: here they were strictly insisted on. Getting up in my insomnia, I would see the double row of beds each surmounted by its ghostly box or funnel, as though the inhabitants were dead and strangely immured – or, perhaps, undead, capable like myself of throwing aside their cerements and wandering hungrily into the deep night. Though presumably some drainage had accompanied the felling of palm trees, standing water – breeding ground of the *anopheles* – abounded within mosquito-flight of the mess huts, and a common sight was parties of *askaris* in charge of a naval N.C.O., setting out with spraying apparatus as though on *safari*. Why R.N.A.S., Tanga, was set up is far from clear to me, perhaps always was. The simulation of conditions likely to be experienced combatting the Japanese was surely rather too verisimilitudinous, though it was, of course, a place for training. My tepid commitment to the locale is indicated by my failure to recall whether more than one squadron was in training at the time of my visit. I must say it seems rather lavish of man-power, even by service standards, to send me to talk on I.F.F. to a single squadron.

The speculation also occurs as to how I spent non-lecturing time, theoretically as lightly worked as a university lecturer without seminars or tutorials. Tropical routine applied, of course, so I was free every afternoon. It was possible to get a lift in a regular truck to Tanga, or slightly beyond to a small bay of silver sand where a diving platform had been erected by some club in the bygone days of peace, an apparatus I brought into a crime novel called *Fantasy and Fugue* after the war. Sometimes I was there alone save for fiddler-crabs and the shoals of tiny coloured fish, the shallower water at the bay's edge almost too warm, bathing of a luxuriousness excelling even Durban's.

The truck came to the swimming place for the return journey, but I often walked the few miles along the straight, palm-lined, tarmac strip into the town, and caught the truck, or a later one, from there. Tea, and simple but good home-made cakes (queen cakes come to mind) could be had at a small serviceman's canteen, run by a few devoted patriotic ladies. The premises must have had a long club, or quasi-club, history, for in one room was a shelf or two of books including a number in German, with evidence of their survival from Tanganyika's past as German East Africa, a régime ended by the First World War. Then, that must have seemed an antediluvian era, part of my brother's babyhood, my father reading the newspaper over breakfast in the house in Frederick Street, Oldham. Perhaps he had even mentioned the East African campaign, for I had a vague sense of knowing about it: maybe it had merely figured in an adventure serial in *Chums* or *The Boys' Own Paper*, the bound volumes of which I loved so much, especially the former; or a little later I may have read of it in a poem by Francis Brett Young when, at Seafolde House, I began to voyage out on contemporary literature. Now, as I write this, far, far more years have elapsed since those Tanga days than separated me then from the First War: no wonder my recollection of that canteen – curiously, situate on a first floor – is profoundly imperfect.

The English books in the canteen (the word is too gross for those bijou and refined premises) were mainly of similar antiquity – volumes of Nelson's red, sevenpenny fiction: the novels of Henry Seton Merriman, William Le Queux, Jeffrey Farnol. I believe I would not have been above pinching any I fancied, for the quest for reading matter had become as arduous as in shipboard experience. One evening I desperately scoured the beds and bedside cupboards of the sleeping-hut, and came up solely, but with gratitude, with a tattered *No Orchids For Miss Blandish*. The satisfaction of physical thirst was also a problem in Tanga's heat. In the town I patronised the garden of the aereated water factory, conveniently near the truck's return point, where the product was available at tables round a fountain. Odd to see at other tables Arabs in robes, daggers in waistbands, for teetotalism allied to mayhem was in those days unfamiliar, to me at any rate. It was an Arab-tinctured coast: sometimes I wandered through Tanga, but the houses were turned inward – courtyards merely glimpsed, no life on the streets.

I do not remember staying in the town after dark. Was there no attractive restaurant, cinema, late truck back to camp? I daresay I could write a bit about evenings in the P.O.s' mess, though monotonous. The insect life at least was varied, amazingly so: the mess kitten scampered over the floor pursuing beetles as big as clockwork toys, which it ate. Nevertheless, it was thin: the life it devoured (one speculated) parasitic, not nourishing. The routine comes back of walking from the sleeping-hut, through the palms, past the monkeys, to the P.O.s' mess, its lights perhaps already on though the sudden dusk still to descend. I might compose a line or two there; more usually read. Boozing came after the evening meal, its extent depending on the variable supply of beer.

It was probably reading and writing that drew Jack Jolly to me. I cannot say that at first I was drawn to him. He was a 'crab-fat', a regular R.A.F. Sergeant, at some point in his career seconded to the Fleet Air Arm, a thin line of dark moustache and an air of extreme *savoir faire* seeming to put him outside the range of service characters I might get on with. Nothing could have been wider of the mark than those initial impressions. It eventually turned out that he, too, wrote verse – untutored, but with great feeling, even rhapsodic. We found other things to discuss, including the free play of the mind over mutual acquaintances that is an essential of friendship. In other words, we slipped easily into affectionate and amused relations, one of the few bonuses for me of what was overwhelmingly a fairly disagreeable episode of my service life. On the rarish nights when the beer flowed unrationed in the bar, Jack Jolly revealed an outstanding talent for reciting ballads maybe familiar to regular servicemen but new to me, notably a long piece beginning:

The sun shone on the village green,
It shone on poor blind Nell.

Despite the physical handicap referred to, Nell's persona and adventures occupy the whole poem (which, now I come to think of it, may well have mainly consisted of a flashback to her sighted days). A ruthless character, Nell leaves her humble parents at an early age, and prospers illicitly, but

Did she send them goods and parcels?
Did she? Did she f—g a—s.

Though recollection seems capable of accounting for a good proportion of leisure activity at Tanga, memory of working life is riddled with gaps. I remember lecturing in a room with a black-board, which I used; even making a few jokes to try to amuse the aircrew audience. Then some time was spent down at the airfield, presumably servicing the I.F.F. sets, helping with the ASV. When I turn to *The Perfect Fool* I see that there I quite neatly fictionalized the business, using the more interesting parts of actuality, sewing up the ragged ends – but it casts little further light on what really happened in 1943. The five and a half pages devoted to Tanga seem to me among the more successful in the book, mainly through their sketching of the characters of the joss-man, an electrician called Charlie Fowler, and Lieutenant-Commander Theobald.

It may seem difficult to believe, but I do not know – nor do I think have ever known – whether the joss-man (naval slang, like 'jaunty', for Master-at-Arms, disciplinary chief petty officer, rank of Melville's dread Claggart), whose exploits are reported in *The Perfect Fool*, was the chief who had mistakenly called me 'sir' on my arrival. The misunderstanding would seem to jibe with his reputation, established before my arrival (and who else but the joss-man would I be directed to see?), but I cannot be sure. After that initial encounter, if encounter it was, I don't think I ever saw the joss-man again. An Edgar Kennedy-like figure may be conceived. I refer to the great American film comedian, master of the 'slow burn', at one time in a number of Laurel and Hardy shorts; of powerful physique but incomplete mastery of the physical world, particularly of potentially dangerous objects like hammers. It was currently said, when I arrived at Tanga, that a rating had gone to the joss-man and asked for a bar of soap, presumably for his *dhobi*.

This episode had corroded in the joss-man's mind, symbolising for him (and, by reiteration, for others) the collapse of the traditional fear of, and respect for, his office (going back to Billy Budd days and before) and the degenerate nature of R.N.A.S., Tanga, itself. A phrase reported to be frequently on his lips was: 'Me, the joss-man, and they ask me for soap.'

'Charlie Fowler' is quite closely drawn from life. I was afraid, when I embarked on the business in *The Perfect Fool*, that I should not be able to capture the essence of his anecdotal style, invariably resourceful and funny, but I see I brought it off not too badly. The fantasy he expressed of the joss-man, relegated to civilian life after the war, emptying the cesspit of Fowler Grange, is scarcely too great an enhancement of his everyday manner. Like Jack Jolly, he offset Tanga's debits somewhat, and I wish his real name had not sunk through my porous memory.

In the novel, the hero escapes from the tentacles of the squadron commander, Lieutenant-Commander Theobald, by reporting sick, but as to that the fiction is much more pat. I had been troubled for some time with a discharging ear, that in Tanga worsened, perhaps as a result of so much swimming. I decided to consult the M.O., and joined the halt and maimed in an open-sided godown, usually waiting the best part of a morning. Malaria, dysentery, festering insect bites and the like, had turned a large proportion of the station's personnel into casualties, whether more or less had the Fleet remained at Trincomalee, who can say?

'Have you been under gunfire?' asked the M.O., a man younger than myself, probing the dubious ear.

'No, sir,' I said immediately, guilty at having come thus far from the U.K., and into 1943, lacking the experience. Later I recalled that in my look-out tub I had been adjacent to the *Capetown Castle's* main armament, a three-pounder, when it was fired at practice.

In *The Perfect Fool* I blame the M.O.'s messing about for the ear's worsening, a positive pain and deep tenderness developing, though this could be fiction's simplifying and dramatizing process. But the book's vital dialogue on the subject subsequently took place in actuality.

'What have I got, sir?'

'Tropical ear.'

'Is it – serious?'

'No, no. All ears are tropical in the tropics.'

Fairly soon the infection moved, and a sore throat developed that more than matched the tonsillitis and quinsies of my youth. As I sat one morning waiting in the godown it was evident that an 'ear', even tropical, did not cover the situation. My temperature, when taken at last, was 106%, and the M.O. dispatched me to the hospital in Tanga. The latter verb is undescriptive of the process. The truck or van waited anyway until the morning's whole hospital intake had been assembled and then, in the familiar manner of suspect road transport (particularly marked in foreign parts), lingered on while some difference, imperfectly understood by the passengers, about the identity of the driver, even the consumption of his elevenses, was argumentatively resolved. Despite the torrid sunshine, it seemed to me my condition was more bearable if I roamed about rather than sat in the godown. An indifference as to whether I lived or died mercifully stole over me. Perhaps I was the only P.O. in the party: at any rate, I sat up front with the driver, the others shaken about in the back as the vehicle jolted over the sleepered road of the swamp. Indulgently, ·I observed the scene, made conversation – both activities as irrelevant as if in a tumbril bound for the guillotine.

The R.N. had taken over part of Tanga's civilian hospital: in the naval ward the beds were pushed close together, one or two figures known back at camp or in Nairobi lying or tottering about, big-eyed, emaciated ghosts of their former selves, victims of dysentery. Bliss to get undressed and into bed, but I was soon disturbed to have a spinal tap. Later came a massive injection of anti-diphtheria vaccine or serum. Following that, I was told the spinal-fluid test was negative. What I had was presumably merely tropical throat.

I suppose the sensational temperature quite soon went down a few notches, but it did not fall to normal, and the days, even weeks, passed, and I was plainly losing weight. The terra cotta tiles of the ward extended to a verandah, its canopy supported by decorative iron pillars. Wounded or malarial servicemen of the East African Campaign of 1916 might well have escaped there, to smoke their meerschaums or Woodbines, from beds as close then as now. Insomniac as ever, I used to wander out during the night, tiles cool to the feet, sometimes thinking that the place might well curiously constitute the scene of my demise. Though staffed by R.N. doctors and sick berth 'tiffies', the naval section was included by the hospital's civilian director in his regular rounds. He was small, shrewd, authoritative, not English, attended by various acolytes.

One day he stopped by my bed for a word and I diffidently told him I was making no progress.

'You must stay in bed,' he said. 'You must not get out of bed for anything.'

Someone in his entourage made a note, and following the prescribed routine I began to improve. Had I at that time read Festing Jones's biography of Samuel Butler I would have recognized the redoubtable Miss Savage's sound belief that 'the great secret of getting well is not to exert yourself.'

6. Kilimanjaro and Kenya

Of reckless foolhood I am full!

– Wagner: *Parsifal* (trans. Alfred Forman)

After all, I was little more than six weeks in Tanga. Certainly in the result my illness foiled the formidable Lieutenant-Commander Theobald from getting a permanent lien on my services. R.N.A.S. Tanga itself would presumably not be keen to retain an enfeebled supernumerary, though it comes to me that I wrote or got a message to the 'Special W/T Section' in Nairobi demanding rescue. Or merely contemplated doing so, pacing the hospital balcony. Anyway, towards the end of May 1943 I was once more a naval draft of one, routed to Nairobi entirely by rail, via Moshi. The line went roughly north west from Tanga, and then one changed to the line running east from Arusha, through Moshi, joining the Mombasa-Nairobi line at Voi, really not far from the coast.

The avoidance of rusty Albacores was not the reason I welcomed this modest official version of a Robertsonian trip: from the map, Moshi seemed almost in the foothills of Kilimanjaro, that once volcanic pimple on great Africa's countenance I longed to see at closer quarters. I could be classed as an anti-traveller, yet much of East Africa allured me. Is the alluring always in the end frustrating, or is that merely the sense of a temperament unable to suck dry the current moment, perhaps especially its visual side? The Martins once drove me out from Nairobi to view the Rift Valley at – but I forget the place. I gazed and gazed: there was even a mountain in the depth of that continental wound. But one had to come away unsatisfied.

I wonder where I read that for the over-night stay at Moshi passengers could remain on the Tanga-Moshi train. Presumably on the ticket, or possibly a notice in the compartment. What I envisaged were fezzed, night-gowned, softly bare-footed stewards making up couchettes, as on that initial journey from Mombasa to Nairobi. On arrival at Moshi in the early evening there was a general exodus (if the phrase can be applied to the few passengers) from the station along the road to an hotel little more attractive than the *Splendide* in *Savage Gold*. I expect that as so often in my life I was playing the thing by ear instead of seeking precise enlightenment. I must have had the hotel dinner – otherwise why should I have entered the place? – but afterwards I made my way back to the station through the nocturnal-noised dark. The unlikelihood of anyone else taking advantage of the railway company's offer of accommodation must by now have been perfectly plain. The train was discovered, I think in a siding or at some subsidiary platform. Encountering a minor Indian railway official, I explained my purpose. He muttered something unintelligible and passed on. The train was empty and unlighted. I selected a compartment at random and stretched out, to sleep if I could, on one of the seats.

Later, someone in Nairobi told me I could have claimed, from the R.P.O.'s office, reimbursement of the cost of a hotel room had I produced the bill, but of course my action was not the result of poverty or even parsimony, rather arose from too great a respect for rules and authority, evidenced elsewhere in these memoirs, not least in the tolerance of Stalinism. Shyness, too, played a big part in the business; also an unjustified reliance on mankind behaving rationally, especially when so instructed. It may seem odd that these traits accompany a strong non-conformity of thought, a willingness to be in a minority of one, but so it has been. From a slightly different aspect the persona may be seen as that of the Fool, the gormless but intelligent innocent who only learns about life through his enormous gaffes, and even then repeats them. Such was the representation attempted in *The Perfect Fool*. I think it must have been in conversation rather than a review that Julian Symons said (I put his objection too crudely) that he did not really see the *raison d'être* of that novel; that for him it lacked plot. As always, his criticism – as I came to see – had great point: the failure of the book is that it depicts too short a span of the hero's life to justify itself in the genre of the picaresque, and its repeated illustration of

Folly too esoteric an artistic shaping, certainly since the work is utterly naturalistic.

It was possible to have the compartment door-windows open, yet draw up barriers of wire-mesh, the material of old-fashioned meat safes, to keep out mosquitos. I did not discover this device at once: in any case, the windows being down, some of the pests were already sharing the accommodation. What with one thing and another the night was troubled. As soon as was decent, in my code of behaviour, I walked back to the hotel for breakfast, no doubt with the air of one staying with friends in the vicinity, but not wishing to impose himself for meals. A mist hung low: nothing of Kilimanjaro was to be seen, though the general direction of its summit could be deduced from the slope of the land. After breakfast I walked farther up the road, hoping the clouds would break before the Voi train left. The poem 'Today and Tomorrow' (in *A Lost Season*) tells me I looked across rows of sugar cane (perhaps in reality maize) and encountered boys driving goats (possibly sheep, the African breed ambiguous), the animals belled and the boys with long thin sticks, so familiar in Africa. As another poet has said: 'A russet shepherd, his sheep too, russet.' I turn to Margery Perham again for what eventually followed: as usual, she gets the experience down vividly with a few ordinary words:

> I had looked forward eagerly to seeing Africa's greatest mountain and it was a hard blow that the sky had let down a heavy drop-curtain of clouds. I gazed hopefully until I was dazzled. Then I saw I had been gazing too low. With a happy shock I saw that higher than I had dreamt possible, and ice-white like the clouds, the summit shone between a rent, the whole of its slopes and base hidden.

Looking back, it seems that though I had been away only a short time a great deal had changed at Nairobi in my absence, but that may only have been because after the due incubation I fell victim to the mosquitos of Moshi and was sent to the sick bay and thereafter on sick leave. Prose pieces about these experiences have survived, and I print them in the Appendix. Pretty well the whole of the story, 'The Sick Bay', follows reality, unless, as a result of time, the reality has been replaced by the fiction. That it is conveniently available is because it was published in December 1945 and I stuck it in my cuttings-book. It appeared in the first number of a magazine called *Equator* (there was only one more), edited by Dr. Edward Lowbury, then in East Africa with the R.A.M.C., who, through life's circlings, I have come to know in recent years.

Following the tropical throat, malaria left me considerably enfeebled. During its course I had chatted with the attendant R.N.V.R. M.O., who turned out to have been in peace-time practice in the south-east London suburb where I too had lived. Like that of 'Charlie Fowler', his name has regrettably faded from my mind. He asked my why I had not gone in for a commission. I told him of the vocation conferred on me in H.M.S. *Ganges*, and its later renewal by Sub-Lieutenant Lavender. He said he would do something about it. He also put my name forward to the Kenya Women's Volunteer Organization for consideration for sick leave at their expense. The hotel they nobly sent me to was in Nyeri, with a celebrated annexe (not in use at that moment of the war) built into a tree, from which during the night animals could be viewed visiting an artificial salt-lick. Nyeri was under Mount Kenya as Moshi was under Kilimanjaro, though not so tucked in.

Subsequent to this leave I wrote the other item in the Appendix, 'The People Round About'. The piece found favour with John Lehmann, as presumably 'The Sick Bay' did not, and was printed in *The Penguin New Writing* 19. Bringing down from a remote shelf a handful of earlyish *PNW*s shortly before writing the foregoing, and blowing the dust off the club-sandwich so formed, was a curious experience. The differently-coloured paper covers, never robust in wartime, were now as fragile as Dead Sea Scrolls: within, remarkable assemblies of talent. The top one of the batch extracted, number 26, had turned into a veritable anthology of personal connections – a story by John Sommerfield, whom I knew slightly (and admired as a forceful left-wing activist) during a spell in London with law crammers as an articled clerk, when I had published nothing; a story by J. Maclaren-Ross, whom I met on a number of usually bizarre occasions after the war, long before his posthumous fame as Anthony Powell's 'X. Trapnel'; reportage by Giles Romilly (who, as related in *Souvenirs*, borrowed my overcoat – the one prior to the overcoat later figuring in these pages – to report the Norway fiasco, presumably wearing it in Colditz during his captivity), and Keith Vaughan (whose gentle personality and vivid paintings I much esteemed when I came to know them). Among the poets were H. B. Mallalieu, character in *Vamp*, and Edward Lowbury. That by no means exhausts the associations.

PNW 26 was published in 1945, by which time, due to sterility, the added zest of finding my own work in the magazine was no more. *PNW* 19 came out at the end of 1944 when I was at the Admiralty. To give a pattern to 'The People Round About', I made out, as may be seen, that the shot P.O. was in the Nairobi R.P.O.'s office and that I knew him, which was not the case. Obtusely, it never occurred to me that the piece might be read by those who would seize on the truth beneath the slight inventions. At that period, stemming from the Thirties, the story closely allied to reportage was a compelling art-form; carried off, indeed, with masterly effect by Julian Maclaren-Ross. To my anxiety, a letter came to me out of the blue, via *PNW*, from the parents of the dead P.O., wanting to see me. In vain in my reply did I emphasise that my knowledge was entirely hearsay, and that the 'I' of the piece knowing the deceased was a fictional twist. They came to the Admiralty from some considerable provincial distance, and I saw them in the duty officer's 'cabin', the only private place I could think of. Distressing not to be able to alleviate their gnawing ignorance. They suspected negligence in the medical treatment of their son, even something unstraightforward about the accident itself: being put on to my piece had renewed their painful and frustrated quest for the truth. Of course, one knew of the force of love, but perhaps the episode betrays a congenital lack in oneself, some unadmirable trait of the unregenerate *littérateur*, imaginative in the wrong way.

Looking at snapshots taken at a not vastly later epoch than my stay at Nyeri, I have been surprised at my corporeal substantiality. The metabolism of comparative youth soon operated to restore flesh and energy. The hotel food was good, quite elaborate, and once they cooked for us as an additional course a trout that fell to the Captain's rod, perhaps his sole catch, the occasion referred to in 'The People Round About'. The wine, too, was excellent, mainly, if not entirely, Australian: surely that could not have been paid for by the K.W.V.O. More memories have been revived by a re-reading of the piece than can sensibly be set down, but I must add a pendant to the business of the gambling machine, which occasionally I played, the Captain much more so, myself watching him. The thing probably took me back to law crammers' days when Gilbert Waller and I played the enticing pin-table for packets of Player's in Charley's caff in Marchmont Street, sufficiently detailed in *Vamp*. I think as many as ten balls descended in the Nyeri machine, all having to be caught to win the jackpot, some modest return being ejaculated for nine and possibly eight. The jackpot had not been won the week of my stay, perhaps not since the war started: its packed *shillingis*, or some of them, visible through the machine's glass front. One evening (could it have been my last?) I financed the Captain, whose skill was far greater than mine, to a final go. Despite mounting, almost unbearable, tension, he caught the lot. Not only did an amazing number of *shillingis* shower forth, but an overflow store was tipped up by the barman with exemplary honesty, though I seem to think its existence had been promulgated as a come-on to potential players. Sensation in the bar: sportsmanlike admission of defeat by Conrad Veidt, a pattern of one of the chivalrous roles played by his prototype.

How did the Captain and I divide the thirty or so pounds accruing? I recall his precise generosity no more than his name and features. He lived in Kenya, his commission being in the King's African Rifles. That is how he came to know Mrs Rickman and so forth. How did he fare in the Mau Mau troubles; under Kenyatta? But the picture is too faded and damaged to perpetuate true interest in its original vividness. It so happens that I have just been looking, as a result of a twist of life later described, at photographs of African and earlier R.N. days, including large groups of ratings annotated with names. One stays blank before few indeed faces or names, though about a good many one would be gravelled to make any enlightening comment. All, if alive, will be bumping seventy – old men with the same astonishing variation of countenance and character possessed in youth.

The touches of local colour in 'The People Round About' throw up the lack of them in these reminiscences, but the deficiency is useful in pointing the nature of memory. I believe somewhere in the house are one or two other very short pieces of story-reportage I wrote when abroad; none published, though I may have sent them out. The two in the Appendix are marginally better than I expected before re-reading them. They are conventional, but at least have got away from fiction's cloying stream of consciousness. They modestly preserve the gains of the novel left unfinished when I was called up, *The Agents*, and look forward to the clarity of the series of four adventure and crime novels I was to embark on a year or so later. Not much interest in this diagnosis for third parties, unless young writers still need telling to refrain from letting their style copy the solemn convolutions of their own concerns.

Thinking about the trout and the Captain's fishing brings back glimpses in the mind's eye of the fast streams, the green rolling country, the background mountains of the Nyeri country I saw with him – country, if not strictly part of 'Happy Valley', which shared that already legendary area's characteristics. For, like Abyssinia and Blackpool, Kenya had a 'Happy Valley': up country from Nairobi, a gigantic unspoiled Scotland; playground and farmland for the amazing race of white settlers who had come into the former Protectorate both before and after the First War. Though James Fox, in his recent book *White Mischief* (1982), remarks with some justification that the murder of Lord Erroll in 1941 and the subsequent scandal broke the spirit of 'Happy Valley', I wish I had had a peek or two at what remained in 1942 and 1943. The Presbyterian Church Hall and the Railway Club were no substitute.

Not awfully long after returning to Nairobi from Nyeri I was told I was to go to Port Reitz, base of the rusty Albacore, to help start a Special W/T Section. At long last R.N.A.S. Nairobi was beginning to break up, the shift east affecting even barrack stanchions like myself. One seemed to be able to look back then to the rise and fall of a whole society. Remote indeed seemed the day when the advance party put up a marquee, episode with strong elements of Edgar Kennedy and Laurel and Hardy, to serve as temporary dining-hall for the main draft still at Mombasa. At that time, and for some time following, we slept in candle-lit corrugated iron huts, near the guardhouse, by the roadside ditches where dead rats were sometimes to be seen. Willie, coming back to our hut after an evening ashore and feeling peckish, had searched in the dark in his jacket pocket for a cake saved from the mobile canteen's mid-morning round (another of the K.W.V.O.'s good works) – and put his hand on a live rat. It being eventually discovered the rats had died from bubonic plague, everyone had to have two, if not three, injections of anti-plague serum, then experimental, perhaps still so. When the frightful effects of the serum had been suffered, the buzz went round it was wholly ineffective. Willie slept opposite me and we discovered that somewhere along the line of our voyagings together our boot-brush polish-applicators had been inadvertently exchanged, as the ineradicable name-marking of H.M.S. *Ganges* showed. We decided not to swap back, and so created a souvenir apiece. My W. E. ROBERTSON brush is still in regular use.

Then Sikh carpenters arrived to build new wooden sleeping-huts farther up the road, squatting on the rafters, white-garbed, white-turbaned. Even in the new huts bedbugs were discovered: they lurked in the folds where the canvas sling met the wooden bed-frame. I must have grown enured to the horror of being nocturnally crawled on. Pyrethrum, a local crop, was a pusser's issue, but proved a deficient bugicide. I recall attacking my bed with a blowtorch outside the sleeping-hut door under the afternoon sun; the place where I might in the middle of the night smoke an hour or so of insomnia away, conscious of the vast, starry sky yet getting to know its bodies and constellations no better than the Swahili language, the educated blacks or Happy Valley. As for a mediaeval peasant or sutler in a Renaissance war, not only did the great events take place beyond my ken but also some occupational or constitutional blinkering cut down the desirable absorption of life's detail in this place that had become rather more than a wayside halt.

I must have been displeased with the Port Reitz draft. The news was also received glumly by the Martins. Yet it was still an amazingly cushy number compared with what might have befallen. However, I think I had done no more than try to prepare mentally for the move when Sub-Lieutenant Lavender's *confrère* came in the iffy hut and said I should be going not to Port Reitz but the U.K. One (or more) of the various efforts to commission me had succeeded, and I had been called home for the status in some way to be conferred. When the news had been imparted I trembled for long minutes. That the frustration of marital and paternal love was to be ended gave a physical shock the like of which I had never experienced before, nor have since. In the magazine *Equator*, opposite the start of 'The Sick Bay', was a poem, rather good, by Edward Lowbury, called 'Port Reitz'. It was evidently written at the end of the war, but is still concerned with the relations of the races, the intrusion of white civilization, in the shape of warships, on an ancient society. The poet makes fascinating the ambience of sea and light. What further and better African poems might I myself have written there?

It must surely have been years later that I learnt that Willie went to Port Reitz in my stead. Probably he told me himself on the occasion I shall later recount. Or I may have heard it from a mutual acquaintance while the war was still on, possibly at H.M.S. *Ariel*. In any case, the knowledge was revived the other day from seeing a snapshot of Willie lying on his bed in his 'cabin' at Port Reitz, annotated thus in his hand on the back of the photograph. He is

77

clean-shaven, in white shorts and shirt, well turned-out; family photographs are on the shelf above, comforting soft drink on the side table. The snap being destined for his wife, he explains characteristically in the caption that the bottle on the shelf is merely the bottom half of a lamp. Undoubtedly he would set up whatever organization was required at Port Reitz with far more authority and effectiveness than I could have done myself.

7.   The Road, the House, the Wife

*One remembers this or that; but to recollect it in the imagination
so as to re-create it – ah, faced with that requirement one finds
the usable, the rememorable past, quite suddenly and drastically
contracted.*

– Donald Davie: *These the Companions*

The penultimate entry in my journal – one of a mere half-dozen
for the year 1943 – is for 29 July: 'Left Nairobi 5 o'clock train
yesterday and landed up here in Mombasa at English Point – tents,
flies on the food, forgotten men – a transit camp'. I cannot stress
too strongly the sense that now constantly nagged of failing to get
home – not as a result of torpedoes or other enemy action but simply
through a breakdown of bureaucratic machinery; or unforeseen
service requirement; or some waylaying, such as suffered by the
journeying protagonists of fairy tales. The sense was exacerbated
by the 'buzzes' preceding any happening to service personnel. I
bathed at English Point, read and even wrote a bit, encountered an
old face or two (the camp was less for newcomers from the U.K.
than for those between ships or shore establishments), and then,
after a few days, I was actually with my gear on the quayside at
Kilindini, awaiting the docking of the transporting vessel. By then
I had an extra item of luggage, a japanned tin box bought along
the way, proof against the depredations of tropical insect life
such as had ruined the waistcoats of the schoolmaster sketched in
Souvenirs. I had painted on it in red (the fluid somewhere available,

79

possibly left over from rehabilitating the Clique's hunting car) PO FULLER FAA, letters to be dimly descried to this day, as though part of a mediaeval fresco.

Where had the ship come from? Massawa? Aden? Lining the rails were many woebegone soldiers' faces, surmounted by those big-brimmed hats one side of which seems to be permanently turned up – antipodean troops, I imagined them to be, but in fact the headgear was not so confined. They had had a rough passage round the Horn of Africa. Those tidings would perturb me somewhat, but the further stage to Durban was unsensational. Part of my luck in the war was that though I spent upwards of three months in troopships I was never sick – no more than occasionally feeling 'that queerish sensation', mentioned by Sir Walter Scott in his journal, when 'we landsfolk . . . without being in the least sick . . . are not quite well'. I am sure I am not a specially good sailor: simply, the weather was never outrageous. That voyage from Mombasa to Durban was like breaking into a novel or play halfway through, relationships advanced but slightly enigmatic, one's own attention and interest hard to engage. What seemed to me then an elderly nursing sister was cavaliered by a much younger proletarian sergeant, that apparent strangeness of the evidently strongly erotic bond denoting my residual romanticism. One precise image of the voyage has survived:

> Last night between the crowded, stifling decks I saw a man
> Smoking a big curved pipe, who contemplated his great wan
> And dirty feet while minute after tedious minute ran.

The lines are a verse from what I suppose is the best poem I wrote during the war, or at any rate the least spoiled, one of a few written in South Africa on the return journey. As to the African poems in general, some critic has pointed out that the oppressed and beautiful animals and blacks stood in quite well for the proper imagery of 'war poetry', but I was never a 'war poet', even in the category of John Pudney, who wrote about courage and casualties somewhat at second-hand, not that there was basically anything amiss in that. I was struck, just before setting these sentences down, by what Professor Richard Ellman said in a discussion with the poet Craig Raine, that, to put it baldly, though James Joyce could not be called a political writer 'he always retained a political feeling'. If the analogy is not too bathetic, I would say politics underlies my African poems, though the political feeling came not from any sort of participation but simply from the wireless and *The East African Standard* and the hangover from Thirties days.

I ought also to take the opportunity here of emphasising what has already been touched on but may have been forgotten in selective narration, the process of what I called, in an African poem, being 'systematically and sickeningly' bored. Donald Davie, in his autobiography *These the Companions* is excellent about the way newly-trained or newly-arrived naval ratings were during the war excluded from real work, at least in shore establishments. Moreover, I was unused to lavish manpower supply, the Great Pyramid Syndrome it might be named, despite my bridge-playing articled clerk days, and a season of office-cricket as assistant solicitor. The leisurely pace of proletarian work, when continuously available, was also something impossible to become accustomed to. I am now apt to say, with truth, that I am never bored. Though shortage of unexpired life has something to do with this, I suppose the claim is fundamentally arrogant, like Pachmann's, eccentric concert pianist of my youth. 'But aren't you bored, M. Pachmann, with all the travelling you have to do?' 'No, no. You see I am always with Pachmann.' But I was bored during the war.

The 'wan and dirty feet' poem I wrote in Durban, the equestrian statue romantically referred to in the first part being some monument on the seafront to a South African pioneer, or perhaps warrior. Almost unbelievably, we went from Durban to Cape Town by train, presumably because of the shortage of shipping: elsewhere, Sicily was being captured, and so forth. The crowded train stopped at stations with household names – Ladysmith, Bloemfontein, Kimberley. We never 'did' the Boer War at school, so the names must have been imprinted by stories and reminiscences in the periodicals read in boyhood: after all, when I was born that conflict was only a decade in the past. On the outward journey I had heard Smuts, transmogrified into a great leader of the Empire, speaking in Durban's main square, while here under station boards bearing the old battle names the generous South African ladies had spread trestle tables with free food and drink for the enemies of yore. Little wonder that despite the heroism in the Mediterranean and on the Russian front, the poem feels that in its epoch wan and dirty feet are more enduring than bronze effigies.

By the time Durban had been reached, Petty Officers Pogson

and Bridle had well and truly come into my life. In fact, I may have encountered them at English Point. They were two of the solo whist four I was a member of, that played every night of the voyage from Mombasa to Durban. The fourth has gone from recollection, probably through guilt, for he was the least skilful player and consistently lost – sums that even for the small stakes played for added up over the sea miles. The games went on so late I was able, when they were over, to open my hammock on the mess table that had been their arena – long abandoned by other games players and letter-writers, disliking the cocooned effect induced by a slung hammock, rather as if one were on the stage to becoming a giant cockroach, like Gregor Samsa. Before turning in I would take the few steps through the black-out baffle into the star-lit air of night, amazingly fresh after Pogson's perpetual pipe and our own fags. Probably I would stay no longer than to pee illicitly in the scuppers, though conscious that here, in a sense, was the real world, the world of poetry; certainly a world I should never plumb and be lucky in any great measure to depict.

Pogson was an experienced solo player, and I had long years of bridge behind me. Bridle, though rejoicing at the fleecing of the mysterious Fourth, must also have been a loser in the long run. Pogson and Bridle were Supply Petty Officers. What Pogson had been in Civvy Street I do not recall. He seemed to me quite old – grey haired, plump; with the neat habits and quiet relish of life possessed by many plump men. His being long-married, even perhaps with adolescent children, did not exclude a professed interest in the side of things more appropriate, as I then thought, to a younger fellow – though the amatory was not a trait of his to be emphasised. A strange obscenity was ever on his lips, the syntax of which I sometimes pondered: 'You wouldn't f— it, would you?' He would certainly have considered his wisdom in other departments of existence equal to that he displayed playing solo whist: but the erotic knowingness was doubtless to emphasise his more general *savoir faire*.

Bridle was a Lancastrian, in pre-call-up life something to do with publicity – the vagueness now expressed very likely emanating from himself, for he was younger than Pogson, could scarcely have attained much eminence in the realm of advertising or whatever it was. He was short and lean, small teeth giving a sense of toothlessness; assured about all matters, despite any deficiencies of know-how inadvertently revealed; longish brown hair, parted low, quite well-brilliantined. Not seldom he might a trifle flashily overcall Pogson's sound bid of 'solo'. Pogson would say round his pipe-stem: 'You wouldn't f— it, would you?' Then at least one knew that what the phrase meant in that context was a sibyllic prognostication of disaster. (The other day, quite by chance, I discovered the phrase in Eric Partridge's *A Dictionary of Slang and Unconventional English*, which may well also list other jests and obscenities cited in these pages as more or less novel.)

The solo winnings went towards a few quite epicurean dinners in Cape Town, when Pogson's carnal relish, Bridle's assumption of vinous discrimination were well displayed. Which of them chose Van de Hum, the South African liqueur then surely little known outside its country of origin, to go with our coffee after the Cape white and red? The brandy of the country we drank with ginger ale as an apéritif. Despite the sensible restaurant tariffs and the staggering cheapness of the booze (ninepence sticks in my mind as the price of a b. and g.a.), Bridle had fairly soon to cry off such outings, and Pogson may well have been glad to see them end, though never destroying the impression of possessing resources beyond his service pay (and winnings at penny solo).

The transit camp was in a western suburb of Cape Town: wooden huts straggling up a small hill of red earth; parade ground and administrative buildings at the bottom, by a railway siding; not near, but in sight of the moods of Table Mountain. The shifting population was fell in every morning to be assigned daily jobs, of a generally dubious nature. When I first arrived there was much skulking in the huts at this juncture, so that the unusual and preremptory command of 'Clear Lower Deck' began regularly to be piped, reinforced by the Jaunty's minions flushing out the huts. Even then, some skulking went on: I remember going up into the hillocks above the camp and playing cards with a few other outlaws (Act III of *Carmen* comes to mind) until the various working parties had been marched off parade and a semblance of quiet had descended. But even this escape route was soon cut off, and one had to parade regularly.

Jobs befitting Petty Officers were rationed out, spread thin. At first it seemed never to occur to authority to enquire about one's trade, so that a little time elapsed before, in my capacity as radar mechanic, I was instructed to walk – and given an approximate bearing – over the hill, where I would find useful temporary employment on some electronic activity there taking place. I should interpolate that just before this, I had encountered in the street in Cape Town a boy known from Lee-on-the-Solent days, if not earlier; good-looking, well-spoken, Public School. He was wearing a white ribbon round his cap, indicating officer-cadet status. It turned out he was not only training in South Africa for a commission, and so not to get to the U.K. on that account, but also, though like me to be a radar and radio officer, his course was the decimating ordeal undergone by potential executive branch officers, even more arduous (he claimed) than its English equivalent. My blood ran cold. Always reticent about the reason for my being on a U.K. draft, after that encounter I clammed up completely.

Higher even than where the card-playing skulkers lurked was a road that eventually ran along a neck of land with the sea close on one side, the orientation of the route unclear in the absence of a map. Fairly soon I came to a newish concrete building overlooking the water. Stores of some kind were being moved into it by blacks. If R.N. personnel were evident their nature and numbers have gone from mind. In the building itself I found a naval officer unpacking crates of unfamiliar but obvious ship or shore radar gear. I could easily invent a plausible persona for him – stocky, Yorkshire, unlit pipe clenched in reliable jaw – but the fact is his appearance is just beyond the limits of memory. When I told him my trade and whence I came he was surprisingly, even startlingly, joyous. He told me what he was setting up, showed me round, assuming in me a knowledge of equipment far wider than ASV and IFF. He was chronically short-handed, I was just the man he wanted, a godsend. I explained I was not in some drafting pool, emphasised my transitoriness despite the shortage of shipping, but nothing cooled his warm anticipation of our collaboration. Literary parallels struck me almost at once: the Old Man of the Sea; Tony Last's encounter with Mr Todd.

By the time the explanation and tour of the building's meagre attractions were over, it was time to return to camp. We worked tropical routine, so the question of the afternoon did not arise. In any case, I never went back. For some time it nagged me that the officer might get in touch with the camp and ask for me, even contrive to get me actually drafted to his radar beacon or training station or what the hell he told me it was. In that event how tragically apt the opening words of the song often sung where matelots gathered at play:

Oh I wonder, yes I wonder,

Did the Jaunty make a blunder
When he made that draft-chit out for me?

On the morning parade I kept mum about technical skills, and
soon became petty officer of one of the naval patrols. My half-dozen
men, a motley collection, were issued with armbands and batons; I
with an armband and whistle. The Fred Karno nature of the force
is thus sufficiently indicated, but there was an added factor, never
fortunately with material consequences, and that of course was my
own unfitness for the assignment. Several members had been on the
patrol before, and had strong notions of where it should deploy.
We were conveyed by coach to some nearby urban centre where
naval personnel might be expected to do mischief, and there I fell
in my men, in two's, to march about like a Gilbert and Sullivan
chorus, of second touring company class. Some film buff among
them directed our steps to an Indian cinema, where we were
admitted without question or payment, a prophylactic against the
vociferous naval critics doubtless feared by the management. We
stood along the barrier at the back of the stalls and watched a film
in the genre then (perhaps even now) all the rage with Indians but
as incongruous as if the Norse deities should appear among the
Canadian Mounties of *Rose Marie*. Another port of call was what
may be described as a large sub-post office, a pinball game and soft
drinks its attractions – the sale of postage stamps and suchlike
presumably having ceased at that time of night, even though it was
run by the hard-working Indians. That, too, was an orderly place,
despite a few sailors mingling with the more or less exotic customers.
Later, one or two of its members led the patrol up an obscure lane
to the backs of some houses, which were, however, quite substantial.
The purpose of this manoeuvre was to chat up a very good-looking
coloured girl, who seemed utterly *comme il faut*; contradicting a
few insinuations before we got there. She was a housemaid or
nursemaid; offered modest refreshments, which some accepted.
Strange insight into the proletarian version of romance, perhaps
always lapsing into crude language and desires.
    Thus such evenings wore away, my thoughts quite often on their
absurd nature, and the preposterous human conduct, from highest
to lowest, that had caused and sustained them. Weariness afflicted
the patrol before its task was done, the final act being to attend the
place where the coaches could be caught back to camp, even more
than an Indian musical the likely background of trouble. We did

not always wait for the last potential disorderly drunk to depart, but took care to secure coach seats for ourselves in good time – I seem to think slipping armbands off to blend with the other passengers, though concealment of the batons would present a problem. Back at camp, the equipment, such as it was, returned to the Guard Room, I was free for a couple of nights, duties being no more than one on, two off, if that.

Miraculously, there was a library in the camp, actually containing a number of readable books. In Nairobi I had been impressed by Karen Blixen's *Out of Africa*, which dealt with the White Highlands at a period which, after all, was no great distance in the past. In the camp library was her pseudonymous *Seven Gothic Tales*, a title I had known since the book came out in the mid-Thirties, but which had never attracted me. Now I read it and was transported. The poetic afflatus of East Africa had not quite left me and the book inspired a poem, 'The Emotion of Fiction', for which I used to have a soft spot. The genre – depiction of the enigma of life, no less – in my case usually resulted in clottedness, but here some air seemed to be let in by the Yeatsian three-beat line. The soft spot does not now remain, nor does any real enthusiasm for 'Isaak Dinesen' – at least for her later stories, when I dipped into them not long ago.

I should have been surprised, presumably disagreeably so, had I been told in Cape Town that except for a piece or two written in transit, a short sonnet sequence quickly composed after getting back to the U.K., and a few small poems as the war ended, my career as 'war poet' was over. It was the price paid for becoming 'chair-borne', as the word was; a sacrifice I was not conscious of making at the time, needless to say. But whatever my eventual fate, I ought to have written more poems in Cape Town. There proved to be plenty of time. The weeks passed and still we did not shift, though buzzes abounded. Then one day a train came into the siding at the foot of the camp for the U.K. draft. With what energy did one bring one's items of kit down the hill, and pile it up, and help with the loading! By that time my baggage consisted of kitbag, hammock, cap-box, tool-box, green suitcase, the PO FULLER FAA tin box, and a substantial cardboard carton. One's personal gear was, of course, in the attaché case issued to naval ratings, and always carried by them outside captivity. The carton was for those 'rabbits' that could not be crammed into the other receptacles, and I use the term not in the strict sense of H.M.'s stores or uncustomed goods to be smuggled through dockyard gates (as explained in *Vamp*) but as indicating things likely to be valued by the rationed civilians to whom I was returning.

The laborious stages followed of getting all this gear off the train and into the troopship waiting at the Cape Town quayside. Excitement was tempered by the unsatisfactoriness of the quarters assigned to petty officers; probably other facilities also were below the modest par of a trooper. Whatever protests were made were of no effect, and eventually the floating hell cast off – then, within swimming distance of land, dropped anchor, presumably waiting for a convoy to assemble. There she stayed the night, the next day returning to the quay, where we disembarked. In due course I found myself carrying in relays up the hill of the transit camp – whether to the same hut or not recollection boggles – attaché case, kitbag, hammock, cap-box, tool-box, green suitcase, tin box and rabbit carton; rather like a practical version of the game of memorising a continuously added-to list of words. Despite a renewal of the helpless and depressing sense that the U.K. might never be reached, nothing so serious as the Sisyphus myth was invoked; rather *The Music Box*, that film where Laurel and Hardy repeatedly haul a piano up a precipice of steps.

In the end, of course, the gear was loaded on a trooper that actually set sail. Though Pogson and Bridle were of the company I do not recall playing a single game of solo. They had become the Supply P.O.s involved in the ceremonies and mysteries of the daily rum issue. The phrase for the call announcing to the hands that the rum ration was available was 'Up Spirits'. When these words were uttered, there was usually someone to add (like the *sotto voce* invocation 'God Bless Her' from old patriots after the toast 'The Queen'; or, perhaps nearer the mark, with inverse piety, as if a response in the Adversary's prayer-book) 'Stand fast, the Holy Ghost'. The elaborate rum regulations were designed to avoid pillage by those in charge, and hoarding and excessive inebriation generally by the recipients. Forbidden, for example, was the practice of sharing one's tot – 'sippers', as colloquially known. 'Neaters' (neat spirit) was, like some rare element or particle, designed by Authority not to exist in free form except transitorily, or under conditions of security. In theory, the precise amount of rum to be drawn and watered, and so converted (the word of the miracle at Cana comes readily to the pen) into grog, was calculable from the daily muster sheets (all the easier at sea, where the population remained constant except for any sick or on jankers or fallen

87

overboard) so that there was no cause for an undistributed residue, let alone for any such to be quaffed by the administrators, as properly happens at Holy Communion. Despite all rules and precautions, it was soon apparent, particularly in Bridle's case, that surplus grog, even neaters, was available for the acolytes. But I have the feeling that Pogson and Bridle did not pass the whole of the voyage in an alcoholic haze. Were they, if the fortuitous pun may stand, rumbled? Did the rum give out, like the food? I doubt if the truth is anywhere recorded, for, of course, on this last lap I had suspended what had been a series of more or less daily letters home, knowing that the paper would get there no quicker, nor more surely, than the flesh.

Like the members of my Cape Town patrols, the P.O.s on board were a job lot, including a few tough eggs, notably a submariner stoker, whom I liked but was never exactly easy with. In charge of the naval draft was a rarity at that time of the war (for me, at least) a Commander, R.N.V.R., his wavy stripes like a border round a carpet. The voyage from Cape Town to Glasgow took six weeks: as conditions on board deteriorated, the P.O.s got more bolshie. The crisis arose over morning boat-drill. The P.O.s, gathered as in a Shakespearean stage direction, on another part of the deck, refused to attend the daily business of falling-in with life jackets and being counted until some demand – now gone from mind – had been met. A go-between took messages to and fro. At last the Wavy Navy Commander, who had previously shown himself capable of giving a good impersonation of a naval pig, intimated unambiguously that if the P.O.s stayed away they would all, every man jack of them, be on a charge. Of mutiny? Who knows? Most, after some rhubarbing, caved in, including myself. Quite apart from native timorousness, which it would have needed greater ideological involvement in the dispute to overcome, I clearly saw that a disciplinary black mark could dish in my commission. The submariner, for one, would have stuck out, even the possible loss of his hooks seeming to mean little to a man who had descended to the depths of Davy Jones's Locker and returned.

Yet I don't know that being commissioned (given getting back to the U.K.) meant much to me, except that by now I certainly at times envisaged myself appearing in naval officer's uniform in the odd places where some sensation would be caused: down the Blackpool street where Kate was then still living with her parents, say, or in Booth's Café, which my mother regularly frequented in common with such Blackpool notables as Mrs Spence-Ormerod. Vanity of vanities; all is vanity.

We stood off Libreville, then in French Equatorial Africa, but there was no shore leave. If supplies came aboard they were not seen in the P.O.s' mess. We put in at Gibraltar. In that pre-air-holiday epoch, the Rock was still very much foreign parts, as familiar from photographs as the Sphinx but seeming no nearer home. We had a few hours shore leave, watch and watch about. It was early November, the weather was like a nice English summer's day, and the town seemed a smaller Chatham or Portsmouth, dubious beds and meals available, goods displayed of a kind one could do without. The atmosphere came back a quarter of a century later going into a bar in Sliema on holiday in Malta, where a photograph of two P.O.s at a bar table commemorated, according to the inscription, the record number of Blues (the vernacular name for a Maltese bottled beer) consumed at a sitting – a total even Pogson and Bridle I doubt could have approached.

At Gib we joined something of a convoy. I wonder (James Fox's *White Mischief* still in my mind) if Sir Jock Delves Broughton was aboard one of the ships, for he, too, got back to England in November 1942 from Nairobi; docking at Liverpool, however, where he soon committed suicide. It seems, though acquitted of the charge, he was actually guilty of murdering Lord Erroll on the Ngong road; that had happened only a year before the road had become familiar to me. After Gib we were soon driving through rain, once again in blue serge and sweaters. The menu for the mid-day meal was now confined to slices of a tasteless species of large poloney, which one day the P.O.s hung on the hammock-hooks round the mess, bizarre protest of some surrealist mass unconscious. An aircraft appeared, disconcerting for a moment, then seen to be a Sunderland of Coastal Command (or so the identification returns promptly to the mind); next a green rim of Ireland, and in due course Ailsa Craig.

> The grey waves rise and splinter:
> We voyage into winter.
> Beyond the disc of sea
> Stretches our northern country.
> Our blood made thin by burning
> And poison is returning.
> Is it too late, too late,
> For dreams to approximate?

Will the port be the same,
Or have another name:
The road, the house, the wife,
Only a spectral life?

How far such lines, written as we hit the British November,
were poet's play-acting, impossible now to specify. Certainly at first
the Glasgow quay had a strange air: uniformly white faces; puddles
and shining cobbles; a squalid wooden hut with a slatternly girl
serving rotten food to the dockyard mateys. As to the last-named,
following my unflattering description of them in *Vamp*, Lady Violet
Powell reminded me of their classic embodiment in song, though
even between us we may not have got the words quite right, the
rude ones worsened by me:

The dockyard mateys' children
Sit on the dockyard wall
Watching their bastard fathers
Doing, it seems, f— all.

And when those children grow up
What will those children do?
Why, sit on their great fat arses
And just do f— all, too.

Though I had been out of England less than two years, on my
internal time-scale the present dockyard mateys could easily have
been the offspring of those observed in the Chatham of 1941. During
the interminable wait on the quayside I telephoned my mother:
Kate's parents were not on the telephone. The ensuing procedure
was that everyone would have to return to his home base before
going on foreign service leave, so I was faced with a journey to Lee-
on-the-Solent and back up to Blackpool, the mileage daunting
enough but less so than the possibilities of bureaucratic sloth and
whim attending the process, as though one were serving a vacillating
and malicious emperor of Rome's decline not the agreeable George
VI. There were hours of anguish, but it was really not overlong
before I was travelling from Lee to Lancashire with Fred Bridle.

It strikes me now as curious that he, too, was from the relatively
small F.A.A. branch. But thus it was; and I have observed elsewhere
in these memoirs that even the entire R.N. provided a society like

that of a Powell or Proust, where coincidence was an ever-surprising commonplace. Readers of *Vamp* will know how in young manhood I was somewhat in thrall to the eccentricities of a friend, Gilbert Waller. Journeying up wartime England with Bridle rather brought back those days, though the prospect of being united with Kate and Johnny induced a euphoria that gave my own character fleeting Wallerian or Bridlian traits. When we reached London, some hours remained before the departure of the Blackpool train. There was time to dine, but instead of making for Soho, several of whose restaurants I knew from pre-call-up times (though the most familiar, the excellent and astoundingly cheap Chez Durand in Dean Street, had perished in the blitz), I took Bridle to the Regent Palace Grill-Room – if, indeed, his provincial feet might not have found it of their own accord. We probably both had the urge to discover in ration-bound London an echo of our Cape Town dinners, which had tended towards hotels; also Piccadilly Circus would be an easy taking off point for two disoriented boys in blue later on.

My brother, whose first step in his hotel training was to serve as what he called a scullion in the Regent Palace kitchens, used to emphasise the scrupulosity and know-how of the meat buyer for the J. Lyons & Co. hotels (among which the Regent Palace was numbered), evidenced when he went with him to Smithfield in the dawn. On family visits to London we always used to have bed and breakfast at the Regent Palace, dining in the grill-room, pricier and said to be superior to the dining-room, where a long *table d'hôte* repast was served. If I may go on, with references only fully meaningful to readers of previous instalments of these memoirs, it was a grill-room meal that my schoolfriend Leslie and I sacrificed for the promenade concert the night my mother and Leslie's were baffled by the film *The Cocoanuts*, at which my brother's falling into the aisle with merriment was probably helped by his being well-lined with steak and chips and pêche-melba – typical choice; improvement on the sausage and chips and vanilla ice of the Blackpool Hotel Metropole grill-room, Hobson's choice of our boyhood. Once when I was at the Regent Palace with my wife-to-be, articled clerk days I suspect, for enthusiasm for the Turf still burned, we went to Alexandra Park, a course now no more, on a chill and rainy afternoon at the fag-end of the Flat. In the penultimate race, following the principle of the 220 System, I backed Taj Ud Din, a horse that had won last time, or last time but one, out. It won again at the generous odds of 10–1 (perhaps even 100–8), my half-crown each way paying the expenses of the outing, with cash to spare. Afterwards, bathed and changed, with what zest did one descend to the grill-room, where even the cabbage seemed delicious, a dish I used furtively to transport in envelopes from Seafolde House Sunday lunches.

Surely memories such as these were revived as Bridle and I dumped our luggage in the mahoganied cloakroom. Puzzling, what my impedimenta consisted of at that moment. When going on leave ('leaf', as always pronounced in the Andrew) hammocks could be left in the hammock-store, and similar facilities existed for tool-boxes. I must have likewise deposited my kitbag and the red-lettered tin box, for I could not have carried more than attaché case, green suitcase and the heavy cardboard carton of rabbits. Actually, it was from Bridle's rabbits that a couple of oranges were produced for the grill-room waitress who had served us – fruit then as rare as that guarded by the Hesperides. More than one motherly figure (waiters and younger waitresses all doing National Service) looked fondly after us as we left, convinced we were home after enemy-destroying voyagings, Bridle not discouraging the illusion. What wartime restaurant makeshifts did we eat? More to the point, what did we drink? Details have gone, but I associate the struggle to Euston in the blackout with euphoria, and in the train we took charge of an empty first-class compartment, pulling down the blinds, tying together with a scarf the handles of the centre-opening doors that gave on to the corridor. Before the train departed, a few individuals (whether first-class ticket holders or frauds like our-selves, who knows?) challenged this uncanny reservation of accom-modation, but the scarf held, and no official appeared. We stretched out opposite each other on the seating, and slept. Blackpool was reached in the early morning, Bridle having departed a station or two before. Miraculously, there was a workman's tram outside the station. Anticipation sustained the carrying of the unwieldy baggage the tidy step from the nearest tram stop to the house overlooking Happy Valley. My mother-in-law, not yet dressed, let me in. Kate and Johnny were still in their beds, so I went up to them.

8. A.S.V.X.

Ariel: Sir, all this service
        Have I done since I went.
Prospero: My tricksy spirit!
                                        – *The Tempest*

In my absence my wife and son had been having a thin time.
Tonsillectomies were still fashionable, and my mother (perhaps
forgetting the operation on me had been twice unsuccessful) persuaded Kate to follow medical advice and submit Johnny to the
knife – not, as in my latter case, on the friendly dining-table but
in the strangeness of a nursing home. A far, far worse subsequent
ordeal was the poisoning of his whole system immediately following
the extraction of a tooth under gas. For a week he subsisted on
glucose and water, his life at issue.

These events, rationing, the strain of being a lodger in the house
she had been brought up in and grown out of, told on Kate's health.
On my foreign service leave we had little notion of what my
movements were to be. Presumably I should have to do a course as
a commissioned officer or probationary such, but where I knew not.
In the way of the Services, things were not much clearer to me
then than they are now, forty years after. Plainly, for safety and
convenience Kate and Johnny would have to soldier on in Blackpool,
though we talked about looking for accommodation of their own,
extremely hard to come by in a town where the R.A.F. was trained
and to which Ministries had been evacuated. At least Johnny was
happy at the kindergarten I myself (and my brother, and, indeed,
Marston, singer and player of 'Vamp Till Ready') had attended
twenty years before. Though the headmistress of my time, the

93

powerfully refined Miss Moorhouse, was dead, the school was run (an odd effect of time, it now seems) by two mistresses who had taught me – Miss Proctor and Miss Arnott, both sterling characters, whose visages and physique I can clearly summon up as in the days, not merely of my son's wearing the white blouse and horizontally-striped black and white tie, but also of my own. Miss Proctor had been music mistress when I attended; as joint proprietor took in more general things. She said to Kate, of my son, aged five or six, that he was almost *too* bright, merited the best possible education; not the only memory of her insight.

Returning to Lee after foreign service leave, I went straight on to an overflow camp at nearby Bedhampton, presumably the overflow established at Seafield Park having itself overflowed. The war had changed from a somewhat amateur affair on Britain's part – the spirit of the game, good losers, and all that – to an affair she was going to help to win. The transformation had been brought home one day by the appearance in the Cape Town transit camp of a body of Commandos (term then quite novel and strange), lumpen-proletarian barbarians, as they seemed, actually carrying knives. Even the standards of war could deteriorate over the years – or so I had thought, as their great boots and loud voices, and red, boily faces arrived in the mess, and dominated it. Despite such experiences, I suppose I never entirely lost the sense that the frightful transit camp at Liverpool, troopships themselves, mines, killing and maiming one's fellow men, were aberrations; that the war could be won or outlasted simply through endurance. Of course, my verse reflects the hopelessness and horrors of armed conflict: the nine sonnets I wrote in that December of 1943 at Bedhampton – a new camp of Nissen huts along a bleak road out of Portsmouth – are still evidence of that, perhaps too much so. When I reprinted the sonnets in my *Collected Poems* of 1962 I made some revisions that I see now are not all beneficial, though whether that is of the slightest interest I do not know, finding the sequence difficult to judge. It is full of notions that went on preoccupying me (such as the feeling in and behind the more sordid departments of existence) but previous Marxist beliefs (such as the inevitable though painful birth of a new society) have ceased to be presented in any simple or straightforward way, or so it seems to me.

Characteristic life at Bedhampton is indicated in the sonnets by references to stoves in the mess, a ramshackle canteen, lights coming on in a shabby cinema, and my working party hacking with rusty sickles the grass and withered weeds of summer. Though *infra dig* for a P.O., I did some hacking myself to alleviate boredom, keep myself warm, and doubtless to demonstrate human equality, despite the sequence taking a pretty cool view of humanity. The camp had not yet developed the size or tradition for daily duties to include interesting items like the servicing of boats or monkeys. But I was not there long, being soon sent on a course, with other P.O. Radar Mechanics, to H.M.S. *Ariel*, a shore establishment near Warrington in Lancashire. Apropos my commission, I am not sure whether it was from Bedhampton or Warrington I travelled to London for a Board. I saw a civilian, Mr Brundritt, quite a famous name in his field, who had come up from the Royal Aircraft Establishment at Farnborough. It seemed to me I did not pass through his questioning very well, or at all. Even those better than I at the craft or mystery of radar might have been hard put to it to discuss theoretical matters so long after passing out as a Leading Hand, and with the limited experience subsequently gained. I would have emerged better from a test on the history of East African exploration, even on tropical disease. I believe Mr Brundritt gave no indication either of success or failure, and that I joined, or returned to, H.M.S. *Ariel* still speculative as to destiny.

At any rate, it was as a P.O. I first went to *Ariel*. The place was remarkable evidence of what could be achieved by an organization that had not hitherto impressed with its alacrity. In November 1941, as Class 1 of F.A.A. trainee radar mechanics, we sat in a Nissen hut at H.M.S. *Daedalus* twiddling our thumbs till the equipment arrived. Now, two years later, a whole establishment existed for the purpose. *Ariel* (one imagines the name chosen by him who chose *Daedalus*, some littérateur of the Admiralty) had been a remand centre, the huts of which had presumably been greatly added to, and brick edifices built. Swarms of young P.O. instructors, by appearance all grammar school swots, had been bred to train the greater swarms of erks, from whose ranks most of the P.O.s had emerged without their setting a foot outside *Ariel*. Above the P.O.s were numbers of 'schoolies', R.N. schoolmasters, who had got up the theory of radio and radar equipment as though it were some traditional intellectual discipline. At the apex of this pyramid, the Commander Training, was none other than Gleave, whom I had seen arrive as a brand-new sub-lieutenant R.N.V.R. at *Daedalus*, and who had put on weight with his extra stripes, even a touch of premature greyness adding to the new dignity.

There was at once an antagonism between the class of P.O.s arrived to start their course, perhaps the first such class, certainly an early one, of P.O.s who had seen service at sea or abroad, and the barrack stanchions of *Ariel*. Even their uniforms differed: as in my own case, P.O.s returned from service had put up gold cap-badges and brass buttons without waiting for their year of acting rank to expire; the resident P.O.s correctly retained their red cap-badges and black buttons. Trouble blew up the first morning. After breakfast, one of the *Ariel* P.O.s (perhaps P.O. of the day) arrived at the hut where the newly-arrived P.O.s were lodged, and ordered it to be swept by the occupants. Shock horror! When had P.O.s ever in naval history wielded a broom? As soon as it was plain the order was going to be ignored, the P.O. disappeared, and there subsequently entered some officer, probably officer of the day, to whom the P.O. had evidently sneaked, in the traditional manner of swots. A longish argument ensued, but it was quickly seen that, quite apart from the question of any individual blotting his C.W. candidature, the position was untenable, for *Ariel* was so stuffed with P.O.s menial tasks were bound to fall to them.

Two strange memories remain of that quite large hut full of P.O.s. The first is of the most persistent and outré snoring I have ever heard, beside which Mrs Parslew's cheese-induced rhoncal sounds (not that I ever heard them), celebrated enough, as touched on in *Vamp*, would have surely been insignificant. The *Ariel* perpetrator was a small, weedy fellow, unnoticeable by day. He was a good sleeper and retired early, so that the initially alarming spluttering and gasping, pretty well continuous, disturbed the first part as well as the dead of night. At the start, one could rely on his neighbours shouting or shaking him out of sleep, for some relief to ensue. But eventually these, better sleepers than I, dropped off, and one was reduced to throwing shoes and paperbacks and suchlike at his bed when exasperation rose too high to be choked back, missiles of limited availability and which had to be searched for next morning. Two or three had been shipmates of his; confirmed the notoriety of his habit. A complaint was put in and I seem to recall acted on, though where solitary, snore-proof accommodation could have been found is mysterious.

The other memory is of lying on my bed (the top one of a two-tier affair, always the better bet) cutting and reading the pages of *The Golden Bowl*. The two volumes of the second impression of the 1923 Macmillan edition, new, pages unopened, had been given to me for my birthday by Kate's brother, Colin. They had probably been obtained by the conscientious Blackpool bookshop, Sweetens, from the publisher's stock; days of the availability and procurement of serious books of the past not yet vanished. My immediate pre-war enthusiasm for Henry James was by no means exhausted, but I marvel now at the pertinacity that drove me through those tough pages in surroundings so inimical. In the process of writing this I get down the very volumes from the shelf and blow the dust off the tops (for I never re-read them, nor surely ever shall) and open the first at the first page of Henry's preface:

> Among many matters thrown into relief by a refreshed acquaint-ance with *The Golden Bowl* what perhaps most stands out for me is the still marked inveteracy of a certain indirect and oblique view of my presented action; unless indeed I make up my mind to call this mode of treatment, on the contrary, any superficial appearance notwithstanding, the very straightest and closest possible.

Then follow the often-quoted words about seeing a story 'through the opportunity and the sensibility of some more or less detached, . . . though thoroughly interested and intelligent, witness.' How the thing brings back my ancient fictive ambitions! Why did I never attempt narration through the sensibility of a detached observer? It might have offset several disadvantages I had as a novelist. And how far indeed is the 'story' of the present work told thus! Disturbed by the thought of these memoirs falling abyssmally short of Jamesian technique (to specify merely one aspect of the business), I take from another shelf his unfinished book, *The Middle Years* (which the flyleaf says I bought in July 1940), and open that to remind myself of the way the Master tackled *his* autobiography:

> If the author of this meandering record has noted elsewhere [*Notes of a Son and Brother*] that an event occurring early in 1870 was to mark the end of his youth, he is moved here at once to qualify in one or two respects that emphasis. Everything depends in such a view on what one means by one's youth – so shifting a consciousness is this, and so related at the same time to many different matters. We are never old, that is we never cease easily to be young, for *all* life at the same time: youth is an army, the whole battalion of our faculties and our freshnesses,

our passions and our illusions, on a considerably reluctant march into the enemy's country, the country of the general lost freshness; and I think it throws out at least as many stragglers behind as skirmishers ahead . . .

One might add, to give Henry's metaphor a literal connotation, that when I first visited her parents' house, Kate's brother was little more than an infant. Before I left *Ariel*, he was to arrive there as a National Serviceman of youngest age, opting on his call-up for the path I had taken, clearer than most in promising promotion and intellectual activity of a kind. He is now an eminent City Chartered Accountant, C.B.E., transformation achieved through mere talent and hard work. Our skirmishing in *Ariel* days would surely have seen dignities of such a kind falling only to the ci-devant Sub-Lieutenant Gleave and the like, men of visibly increasing ponderability; our straggling still in bijou Happy Valley – view of life perhaps little changed.

Besides the multiplicity of buildings and personnel constituting H.M.S. *Ariel*, it also offered a new version of A.S.V. – 'A.S.V.X.' – the mysteries of which I think I am right in saying constituted the main feature of the P.O.s' course I was on. Like the effect of the war on skirts, wavelengths had got shorter: moreover, cybernetic principles had been ingeniously applied to enable radar to 'lock on' to a target, device commonplace now, then a remarkable novelty. The best of the schoolies lectured on this latter development: his description was lucid, gradually unfolding the secret of the electronic machinery that without human intervention enabled the directional wireless waves to track a moving object. When suspense was at its height, I cried out: 'I can't bear it!' – characteristic desire, in and out of season, to amuse. Neither cathartic laughter nor my implied tribute left the schoolie best pleased, but he recaptured his audience in brilliant style, so no harm was done.

Ariel was midway between Warrington and Leigh. The former I never grew to care for in any way: set in the great Gromboolian plain of south-east Lancashire, its air seemingly perpetually gritty, it did not satisfy any nostalgia for the industrial north I then possessed, remote in aspect as it was from the green moorland roped with walls glimpsed from Oldham streets, or (the reverse view) red factory chimneys hazing built-up valleys. I preferred Leigh, usually went there on shore leave, though it was only a small, dark, colliery town. The Salvation Army had added to the sparse amenities by opening a canteen in a tin chapel or church hall at the end of an alley; modest in size and comfort but offering some unusually good delicacy, I think sausages. In both towns I patronized any cinema showing a film not positively awful, and sniffed out emporiums with books to sell.

No more than sleeping ashore, watch off, was possible, so to give us more time together Kate and Johnny sometimes came for a Saturday night in Warrington, conveniently on the Blackpool to London main line. We stayed at a non-licensed hotel in the suburbs of Warrington, perhaps because of its readily available accommodation, how discovered now mysterious. Memorable, the linoleum on the dining-room floor; high tea in the early evening, normally boiled ham (more likely spam, an American import by then despised, subject of comedians' jests, but to me a novelty, thought not bad at all, dried egg in the same category). After that, the patient Johnny would be put to bed, and Kate and I depart for the local pub until the evening ration of short drinks ran out, a period more prolonged than in the central Warrington pubs handy for the thirsty circumadjacent American Army and R.A.F. bases. One marvels at the hope and affection sustaining such crude amusements, so far from one's ideals of domesticity and absorption in art. Even large and superficially quite efficient organizations reveal, when well-known, improvisatory and fallible parts. The sketchy and tenuous nature of small hotels in wartime was almost immediately apparent, but in the end one was always duly thankful for the shelter and sustenance, however odd, that facilitated continuation of private life, however caricatured, when existence was dominated by the State.

A photograph exists, taken by a street photographer near the Charing Cross station of the Southern Railway (as it then was), of Kate, Johnny and me striding along in winter garb. I am still wearing a P.O.'s cap (with gold badge) and pusser's greatcoat. The folder under my arm indicates the occasion: I am off to deliver the typescript of my third book of poems, *A Lost Season*, to the Hogarth Press in the person of John Lehmann at his flat in Carrington House, Shepherd's Market. Plainly I was on leave of some sort, Kate and Johnny down from Blackpool; I would conjecture all of us staying with the ever-hospitable Kathleen and Julian Symons in St. George's Square, Pimlico, at the very top of stairs always surprising by their prolongation of flights, as in a work by Piranesi. In his *Notes From Another Country*, Julian dates their moving into the St. George's Square flat as January 1944, he by then invalided out of the Army. Emerging from the Strand seems a bit of jigsaw crammed into the wrong place: fitted properly, I expect other parts of the picture might have to be slightly altered.

While I was in Africa, Kate had been in constant touch by letter with John, sending him typed versions of poems and so forth, but on one memorable occasion he arrived by taxi at her parents' house and subsequently took her to the Blackpool Opera House (where there was a week's ballet) to see Beryl Gray and Alexis Rassine in *Swan Lake*. 'Built like a carthorse,' said John approvingly of the young Beryl Gray. What he said of Blackpool has not come down. His taxi would have driven along the road that divided Sparrow Park and Happy Valley, but getting on for forty years were to elapse before my memoirs enshrined them. Very tall and handsome, his light brown hair little if at all touched with grey, marked features, pale blue eyes that would narrow less from the smoke of his holdered cigarette clenched in strong jaws than a silent questioning of artistic or other opinions, John was a figure in several aspects quite formidable, scarcely to be envisaged in Blackpool at all, incongruous there through both character and personal history. His ancestry went deep into Victorian letters; his early youth was associated with both Bloomsbury and the Auden School; his sisters were already ornaments of the contemporary theatre and novel. Yet no apparent barrier of class or milieu ever stood in the way of his editorial quest for new imaginative art and literature, or of the bestowal of his friendship. Now I have known him so long, I would want particularly to emphasise his sense of comedy – never, alas, quite to find an adequate outlet in his works (though in recent years he has written well about Lear's and other nonsense) – always lurking, ready to break out into laughter and comment about political, literary and human folly. Such a strong sense, of course, presupposes sharp judgements.

He had written to Kate that he must hold a party for me when I returned from abroad. The portage of *The Lost Season* typescript may well have been to that very function. I wonder now whether I had gained, during the half-dozen years that separated this party from the rather more haphazard one, also in my honour, organized by the editor of *Twentieth Century Verse* and described in *Vamp*, increased know-how in expressing gratitude. I doubt it, but on the second occasion I expect Kate would cover deficiencies, for both she and Johnny attended, the latter making a quiet hit.

100

Could the proceedings have started with tea, merged into early evening drinks? I would like to see a roster of the guests: it might restore one of those set pieces of past life in which one was too involved, however, to have brought away more than an odd room-corner or piece of anatomy. Three men I feel sure were there. Stephen Spender was one, his poetry loved by me, his political attitudes more or less reviled, for upwards of a dozen years. This must have been our first meeting, but not for me the surprise expressed by another 'war poet', Timothy Corsellis:

> I had expected
> That your body would have been small
> Indeed it was necessary for you to be small
> Stature in contrast with ability.

Though as in another existence, it was only a few years since I had absorbed Isherwood's *Lions and Shadows*, where he is unforgettably portrayed as Stephen Savage, 'immensely tall'. What made the most impression in actuality was the voice, as for me it has continued to do, the marked sibilants perhaps stemming from his maternal German ancestry. Philip Toynbee was another guest. I admired his novel *A School in Private*, may have told him so. For a few years thereafter, without being 'friends', we knew each other, would speak, accidentally meeting in bars or bus queues, but even that slight relationship faded, as faded – or, rather, changed into something quite bizarre, so it seemed to me – the talent that had produced the early novels. My relationship with him was fairly typical of relations with a good few whose background and *modus vivendi* were on a higher social (and intellectual, come to that) level than my own, though shyness and my indolence about personal relations (and much else in life) enter the matter just as much. In one sense, the situation was not unlike the difficulties I found in getting on with the working-class in political days of the early Thirties, and, in fact, in the Andrew – as witness encounters with such as Toscanini and Ivanskavinski Skavar. Between more or less high falutin small-talk and the expletive-studded account of mere events, there is (or at any rate used to be) an area of communication occupied by the lower middle-classes characterised by irony, decency and unpretentiousness, and that was what I was used to by birth and upbringing. But I should add, about Stephen, that from then on we met at irregular intervals, sometimes of literary collaboration or social intimacy, without, to our mutual regret, ever really becoming close friends; all the worse for me since few, with a phrase from tongue or pen, can amuse me more.

The third remembered figure at the flat in Carrington House, and seen on subsequent similar occasions, puzzled me for quite a time: a sturdy middle-aged man not above medium height; noticeable spectacles, large head made to look even larger by the thick, straight, grey-streaked hair, despite its being well parted and brilliantined down. Major Morris was the name I eventually correctly attached to him, wondering if he wasn't a financial backer of the Hogarth Press or character from the printing world. In the end, I saw quite a bit of him, for he turned out to work for the B.B.C., then, or soon, head of its Far Eastern Service, for which I used to broadcast at the fag-end of the war and for some time thereafter. He had been in the First War, served afterwards in India as a regular soldier: dress and manner, as well as age, marked him off from the Spenders and Toynbees, but between us was little more than the gentle bantering established with B.B.C. figures seen regularly in the way of business. When I read his *Living With Leptchas* I greatly admired it, but whether I told him so is even more doubtful than in the case of *A School in Private*.

A Lost Season (its title came from Donne's Elegie XII: 'His Parting From Her') must have been published no more than six months or so after the party, time-scale commercial publishers should ponder today. Following the modest but surprising success of *The Middle of a War*, its reception disappointed me, an emotion of publication often to be repeated. Even in the New Stanley lounge, better stuff seemed to be emerging, and at the time of its going through the press it struck me as a stronger book than its predecessor, though the extent of the revisions I made in some of the pieces for my 1962 *Collected Poems* indicated the depth of later dissatisfaction; again, a common sequence of events.

However, when I look in my old cuttings book I see that the reviews of *A Lost Season* were almost without exception friendly, some remarkably generous. As so often, the remark applies that was made by Arnold Bennett in a letter to J. B. Priestley: 'Like all authors, I feel deeply convinced that I am not understood as completely as my amazing merits deserve.' Perhaps disappointment stemmed mainly, if not solely, from a notice, one of the first, by C. Day Lewis, which began with a kind word but failed to keep going in that vein, much preferring Laurie Lee's *The Sun My Monument*, published by the Hogarth Press at the same time as *A Lost Season* and with which the latter was usually reviewed. I may well have known then that Day Lewis and Laurie Lee were colleagues at the Ministry of Information, and so suspected favouritism. I had biffed Day Lewis in one or two pre-war reviews, thus may have been lucky to get the kind word, for some littérateurs have long memories. Both Laurie and Cecil may have been at the Carrington House party: the former I soon came to know quite well, the latter not until long after the war, when he and his wife, Jill Balcon, became neighbours. By that time I was able to judge his work freed from period and theoretical prejudice: for his part, he had established himself more comfortably in the intervening years as, in a sense, a pre-Auden poet – certainly using his own clear voice, without Audenesque ventriloquial turns, probably aided in this by Jill's own clear voice, too.

I see from the cuttings book that the reviewer in the *Glasgow Herald* was one of those to whom *A Lost Season* did not appeal: 'Roy Fuller . . . continues submerged by pain and nausea.' As a matter of fact, although the Bedhampton sonnets at the end of the book still envisage a 'stormy future', I must surely have thought we had moved out of the epoch of 'terrible defeats' (phrase from 'The Petty Officers' Mess', an earlier poem in the book), though envisaging that those for the Axis Powers would lead to social revolution, certainly in Germany, and that would be infectious for some time to come. Possibly not until the early summer of 1944, when the Second Front was thoroughly established, did I dimly discern that my life after the war might not differ drastically from what had gone before. Some reconstruction of my political viewpoint of the time could be made from my letters, but that would surely bring pain and nausea to me now: better be represented by a few vague generalities than the naivetés that might be unearthed.

I was a fair way into the P.O.s' course at *Ariel* before my promotion to Sub-Lieutenant (A) R.N.V.R. arrived, with instructions to report to Portsmouth a week or two thence. Another P.O. was involved in a similar transaction. We were sent on leave instantly, as though the solecism of officers in lower deck uniform and conditions could not be borne by the Andrew. Indeed, the change in status had been marked from the start by the matter being dealt with not by the Jaunty's office but the Captain's – our summoning there effected by the Captain's Messenger, blend of classical and Kafkaesque role I myself had once played, as noted in *Vamp*. On this occasion it inclined towards resembling a supernumerary of the gods (in benign mood), impression augmented by an office complement of white-shirted Wrens amiably serving up railway warrants, advice, etc.

The pieces of paper they handed out embodying our instructions emphasised in terms a nit-wit could not misunderstand that if officer's uniform was not by then possessed, one must report to Portsmouth in plain clothes. My leave was spent in Blackpool, and it never occurred to me to try to get uniform off the peg or even find a tailor who might run the essential items up in the few days available. I knew, probably from their advertisement in the preliminary pages of Volume 1 of the *Manual of Seamanship*, issued to all ratings on joining, that Gieves, the ancient naval tailors, had an emporium in Portsmouth, and that was where I intended to go. I wonder now why I never contemplated patronizing Southworths, the Blackpool tailors with a ready-to-wear department, touched on in *Souvenirs*, particularly as I must have been anxious that the fortnight of the Portsmouth course might not give Gieves sufficient time to exercise their craft. Surely Southworths was still in being, though the ambient world had changed, for they had made the suit I was married in less than seven years before. The Southworth brother in charge of the ready-to-wear side of the firm would have run his fingers under the broad lapels of a monkey-jacket, setting the fit, and murmuring, in the words of yore: 'Very tony, Sub-Lieutenant Fuller. Extremely nutty.'

A slight mystery surrounds the garb in which I arrived at Portsmouth: grey flannel trousers, certainly; and the jacket of the Manx-tweed suit mentioned in *Vamp*. I feel pretty sure these would be worn on the way to join my training establishment, sent back to Blackpool by *Ganges* after the vicissitudes of my kitting-out. By then the suit must have been much less than pristine, the reason I was pairing its jacket with grey flannels (though, as *Vamp* records, I wore the suit after the war, rationing by clothing coupons prolonging its life, without doubt). I could have had in war-time Blackpool little more than the *Ganges*-journeying clothes, so I wore to Portsmouth on my exterior what I had probably worn to Shotley in 1941 – a dark green, single-breasted overcoat bought off-the-peg in a shop called Freebody's in Woolwich, the winter before the war. The colour and style were daring for the Thirties, even their final year; initial hesitation in the shop turning to self-congratulation when I had worn the garment a few times, it seeming the sort of thing a literary man might wear without losing face as a solicitor. Certainly on the Portsmouth occasion the ensemble was topped by a dark brown trilby hat. One might add that, at the moment of writing, an overcoat as such may soon come to need an explanatory footnote, for owing to the proliferation of motor-cars, wool becoming increasingly expensive, and the general acceptance of inelegance, the normal outdoor covering for men is a short or shortish jacket, often with an attached hood hanging down in wrinkles at the back, often made of padded plastic, aciduously coloured.

Some of the officer entry at Portsmouth were complete sprogs – Gleaves of the day, brought in straight from university or industry to stiffen up the technical side of the Andrew. Others had gone through basic general training, but little more, their commissions having caught up with them betimes. Still others were old sweats, or relatively so, among whom I counted myself. Immediately, one was back on the parade-ground, in the gymnasium, the swimming bath, as in *Ganges*. Readers of *Vamp* will know of my experience of squad-drill. This stood me in good stead at Portsmouth, since the emphasis of the short course was on the inculcation of the power of command. As at *Ganges*, I was not displeased with my parade-ground performance, but one day, momentarily halted as we marched round in single file (possibly in that order for some such manoeuvre, needing no practice in my case, as saluting, eyes right or left), the officer drilling us came irritably up to me: 'Haven't you got your uniform yet?'

'No.'

'At least you've no need to wear that hat.'

'I thought it would be appropriate, for the salute and so forth.'

'Not at all.'

I am not sure that the reason given for wearing a head-dress was entirely honest. Since I could not swank in uniform, there was an urge to appear as incongruous as possible, disguising, too, previous parade-ground experience – a sort of hustler instinct. Besides, I had inherited from my maternal grandfather a strong habit of wearing hats, funny ones included. I should say, however, that on the parade ground I refrained from wearing the poetic-lawyer's overcoat. Kipling almost had the appropriate words in his 'Back to the Army Again':

> I'm 'ere in a ticky ulster an' a broken billycock 'at,
> A-layin' on to the sergeant I don't know a gun from a bat;

> My shirt's doin' duty for jacket, my sock's stickin' out o'
> my boots,
> An' I'm learnin' the damned old goose-step along o' the
> new recruits!

I had been measured at Gieves on The Hard by a tailor of the old school who may well have so served those engaged in the action off the Mole at Zeebrugge, the sideshow representation of which had so terrified me as a child. 'Watch-coat or greatcoat, sir?' I hesitated only fractionally: 'Greatcoat.' I was in doubt whether a watch-coat (a shorter affair, cut on the lines of a British 'warm') would satisfy every sartorial demand of the Andrew – an Admiral's visit, say, or an Armistice Day parade. On the other hand, if one could get away with the garment on all occasions, it would, with a substitution of buttons and removal of epaulettes, serve quite well for the eventual return to civilian life. But thrift of that kind, even with a nature inclined to parsimony, was outweighed by the desire to make the maximum impression in naval officer's uniform, and that, to my then way of thinking, required the half-belt and pleat at the back, the mid-calf length, the general Erich Von Stroheim effect, of the greatcoat.

I transferred to the hero of *The Perfect Fool* some of my preoccupation and anxiety about the greatcoat and other items of uniform, when actually acquired. Tempting to go into the matter again, but I can hardly expect from others an interest approaching my own. Gieves made me two uniform suits: a 'working' suit in serge, and a 'best' in more expensive material, probably barathea. Oddly enough, like the jumper of the square rig Number Twos issued to me at *Ganges*, the working jacket was cut somewhat too loosely at the waist and hips, but somehow the opportunity never came to have it altered, and it nagged me slightly till the end. (Yet as I write this it occurs to me that the generosity of cut in the working jacket may have been deliberate, a Gieves tradition to allow greater freedom of movement in such activities as scrambling on to the Zeebrugge Mole.) Another regret was the gold braid round the cuffs. One says 'round', but that was the botheration: regulations had been made that, to save braid, stripes (in my case, one) should go only half-way round. Those commissioned before the regulations had satisfactory full circles; a few had illicitly acquired the same: I had to put up with what always seemed an indication of rank more appropriate to a banana republic navy than the Andrew.

Like Chatham had been, Portsmouth was, of course, grossly overcrowded. I slept in a former hotel on the front at Southsea, requisitioned by the R.N., atmosphere of former modest comfort, present near-subsistence existence, familiar to everyone doomed to such places during the war, most aspects brilliantly recaptured fictionally by Waugh and Powell. Fortunately, meals were taken in the splendid Portsmouth wardroom, resembling a great provincial club. The building was red-brick, perhaps Edwardian, opposite the main gates of the barracks: holding one's pink gin in the anteroom, the various forms of lower-deck life could be seen swarming out on errands of pleasure and duty, bringing back one's Chatham days in a mist of *Schadenfreude*. The food was excellent. On entering the dining-room one asked a steward in charge of a bank of pigeonholes for one's napkin, giving the number of the napkin-ring (the same as its pigeonhole) assigned to one on joining the mess – alliance of gentlemanliness and catering-check possibly dating back even before Zeebrugge. Though there was a choice of pudding as of every other course, always on the menu at lunch-time were cold prunes and rice: the former plump, in an exiguous but flavoursome juice; the latter not a traditional rice-pudding, the grains more articulated, though tender. As I thought about the Portsmouth course, just preparatory to writing about it here, the foregoing delicacy came to mind and, quite moved, I worked it into a sonnet sequence then being composed:

The creamy rice, the prune juice rich as blood.

Even breakfast was taken in the wardroom. I remember dressing in the little hotel bedroom the morning after I had picked up or (I rather think) Gieves had efficiently delivered the final garment enabling me to appear in the role of naval officer. There was difficulty with the stiff, double collar, an item not worn since as a boy at Seafolde House I had graduated from the Eton jacket that had involved an Eton collar (with black bow tie on a stud) to a Marlborough jacket accompanied by stiff, double collar and ordinary black tie – Sunday-wear for boarders. The most effective sequence of operations (opening the collar, affixing it to the back-stud in the shirt-collar, laying the tie along it, closing the collar while it was horizontally extended, etc) came back like riding a bicycle, initial clumsiness soon wearing off. The trouble was getting the knot of the tie to stay in the apex where the collar-ends met. I had acquired the collars in the officers' section of pusser's stores, where they were dramatically cheaper than in the shops, but they proved to be cut too high, with non-existent tie-apertures – another Zeebrugge hangover. Once again, parsimony was shown not to pay in the long run. I fairly quickly bought some collars more conveniently and fashionably cut away, but not until I was able to go to Simpson's in Piccadilly was the problem satisfactorily solved: that excellent shop sold stiff collars cut low at the front with long points, very tony, and with an aperture of perhaps as much as three-quarters of an inch into which the tie-knot would slide and be retained.

That winter's morning, walking in the dark from the hotel to the stop where a trolley-bus could be caught to the wardroom, one felt like a waxwork rather than the juvenile star of a West End naval comedy previously envisaged. The pristine rigidity of the cap, the deficient collar's chill accentuated by the sea air, the embrace of two double-breasted garments, the general hollow insubstantiality of going unbreakfasted into the world – these had most to do with the disappointing first entry in costume, not that such egotistical pleasures can ever come up to expectation.

I was certainly in uniform, maybe just as well to be out of a green overcoat and brown trilby, however dark, when after a session in the swimming-bath the members of the course were hanging about, waiting for the laggards in dressing to join them so that all could go together to the locale of the next item on the programme. At the other end of the bath there appeared, half inevitably, half surprisingly, like some minor Dickens character, the familiar figure of the short, dark, muscular young officer (a pocket Hercules, the phrase in *Vamp*) who almost two years before I had noted with jealous displeasure lording it over the gymnasium at *Ganges*. In the interim he had put up another stripe. With him were some foreign officers, plainly on a tour of inspection. Quite soon (though after a lapse of time sufficient for him to have made a farewell, most likely a temporary one, to his party) he came along the side of the bath and confronted us.

'Who is in charge of you officers?'

One of us (juvenile, mild, deputed to see us on time for – perhaps march us to – our ensuing engagement) spoke up: 'I am.'

'Haven't you been told yet to say 'Sir' when addressing a superior officer?'

Even to a sprog, the novelty of one stripe sirring two would have been extreme.

'Yes, sir.'

Lieutenant Hercules, I dare say encouraged by imagining us all to be newly joined, and by the easy technical back-door, then proceeded to administer a thorough ballocking. We had been lounging about, hands in pockets, chattering, implanting in representatives of the Allied Powers doubts as to the smartness and efficiency of the Royal Navy, not least about the quality of its new recruits. He was minded to report our behaviour to the proper quarters. How pleasing to me the evidence that the shit in manner was a shit in action! Afterwards, I commiserated with our temporary class-leader, disclosing Hercules's cockiness of yore.

Since writing the foregoing I have turned up a booklet which for years I have known lurked near the bottom of a perennially uncleared letter-tray in my study. It is the Pamphlet on Officers' Divisional Course handed to us on arrival at what I see is identified as 'St. John's School, R.N. Barracks, Portsmouth.' I am tempted to reproduce the five aims of the course, printed at the start, but perhaps they can be sufficiently imagined. After them are the following sentences:

To implement the above, lectures are given, brief summaries of which are found in the pages following.
Squad Drill, Physical Training, Swimming Lessons to Non-Swimmers, and A.R.P. duties also find their places in the course.

The swimming-bath visit may well have been merely for the purpose of the instructors there identifying any non-swimmers.

Judging by the length of the pamphlet, we must have heard a good few lectures during the fortnight. The atmosphere was less that of *Ganges* than of Gibson & Weldon, the law crammers I attended when an articled clerk – those lecturers aspiring to humour being sophisticated performers, like L. Crispin Warmington at Gibson's, their jokes far from those perpetrated by, say, the rifle-drill P.O. at *Ganges*. One of them (a tall, dark R.N.V.R. Lieutenant, said to have been in advertising) was good enough for the stage, as they say. I see him, for instance, freezing in the middle of a rhetorical gesture to observe his upraised arm with surprise, and pulling it down to modest normality with the other hand.

One page of the pamphlet consists solely of these words:

Light Weapons

Handling, loading, working and sighting of following arms
is explained:-
    Revolver
    Thompson Sub M.G.
    Lanchester
    Sten Gun
    Description of Mark 36 grenade and sticky bomb

The entry brings back what I had completely forgotten – the day
spent at the Gunnery School on Whale Island, a place of desolation
surely in the best weather, on that drizzling day piercingly cold. A
packed lunch was involved, eaten in some milieu of discomfort, if
not the open air. As in all arms training, there was more hanging
about than firing weapons. I recall shooting off a .303 revolver and
lobbing a grenade, but guess the other items unavailable or not
reached in the time; again, a common enough situation. It strikes
me now (maybe struck me then) how preposterous the notion behind
the day – that I should use the implements against a living target.
The preposterousness would have been increased had the more
gangsterish guns been in my hands. I had never been a pacifist, but
of course by then it was unlikely I should be called on to fire a
weapon in anger. I suppose now, if I were still of an age to be
called up, I would declare a conscientious objection to killing, and
sweat that position out – though the question arises, in a not
dissimilar realm, why one is not a practising vegetarian. To return,
after all, to those 'aims' of the course, perhaps they may be thought
remarkable in never mentioning aggressiveness or the like. Naval
customs and a sense of comradeship; good discipline and welfare;
powers of command and leadership; and (most remarkable of all)
encouraging an 'ideal' (inverted commas *sic*) in life and the ambition
to live up to it – these are what are hoped to be taught during the
fortnight. Again, some lines of Kipling – staggering poet – are not
too wide of the mark:

> The Doorkeepers of Zion,
> They do not always stand
> In helmet and whole armour,
> With halberds in their hand;
> But, being sure of Zion,

And all her mysteries,
They rest awhile in Zion,
Sit down and smile in Zion,
Ay, even jest in Zion,
In Zion, at their ease.

Soon I was back at *Ariel*, embarked on the officers' course, even longer than the P.O.s' course left uncompleted, since it comprised every radar and radio set used in the Fleet Air Arm. Among our numbers now were Wren officers, as novel as undergraduettes in olden days; also, Wodehousian style mingling with Dickensian coincidence, Peter Lavender, with a second stripe up like the pocket Hercules. Initially it was odd to encounter him again on equal social terms, just as it was to move in the heights of *Ariel*, such as they were, after serving below stairs. No risk, even as a mere Temporary Sub-Lieutenant, to be required to sweep the mess-deck; indeed, I had a tiny cabin to myself, though on the whole slept no better.

9.   D.A.E.

Thus Ariel ended.
            – Thomas Hood: 'The Plea of the Midsummer Fairies'

Like Dr. Johnson's Rasselas, my wife longed to escape from Happy Valley. Or, rather, as already indicated, from her parents' house that overlooked the former concave haunt of the pierrots of our childhood. During the Blitz any old port in a storm was endurable. Then, for the first part of my National Service, being mobile with a firm base worked out not too badly. But during my time abroad a place of her own grew to be the sole desideratum: in Blackpool such accommodation was almost as scarce as bananas, for the reasons given. As in many facets of tolerable wartime existence, some illegality had to be embarked on, and Kate enlisted the help of the wife of Rod Davies, her former colleague on the local newspaper, encountered by me with full coincidental force at *Ganges*, as recounted in *Vamp*. Rod's wife had also been a colleague, still worked as telephonist, and she undertook to tell Kate, before the paper appeared, of any likely accommodation offered in the small ads section. At once, by lucky chance, Kate secured a furnished flat. Strangely, the house of which it was a part also overlooked Happy Valley, the longer side of its rectangular shape, so the municipal putting-course and garden, of which it now tamely consisted, once again began to live up to their ancient name.

The accommodation has been described as a flat, but in fact was scattered throughout a house by no means large. Of course, Kate and Johnny were soon familiar with its tenantry and topography, but to me, a not too frequent visitor, some mystery always remained.

The house was owned by Mrs Rosewell, a quite elderly widow: plumpish, white-haired, agreeable, a certain air of scattiness; perhaps had been pretty in her youth. Also in the house, on what terms I know not, was her younger sister, Mrs Slate, also a widow, whether true or grass perhaps in doubt. Mrs Slate could never have been pretty: she came from a bigger and coarser mould than her sister, gave a hint of a man in drag, a pantomime dame. As so often in sisterly relationships (Joan Crawford and Bette Davies in *Whatever Happened to Baby Jane?* come to mind), the underdog, so to speak, dominated. Mrs Slate's dependence on her sister's bounty did not inhibit her from throwing her weight about, and argumentative exchanges were even sometimes heard from those parts of the house retained for the sisters' use (exiguous parts, it must be said, for Mrs Rosewell slept in their kitchen and Mrs Slate in a, or the, bathroom).

On the first floor was the apartment rented by Mrs Cartwright; sometimes with her, presumably when he could get leave, a member of the Polish forces in England whose name was not, of course, Cartwright. As a matter of fact, the consonantal excesses of East European nomenclature often led to anonymity, certainly among Blackpudlians, never noted for articulation – a deficiency particularly deplored by my old headmaster, the Boss; sufficiently illustrated in *Souvenirs*. 'Mrs (or Miss) So-and-so's Pole' might be the only identity given, as though an inanimate object were in question. Mrs Cartwright was nice, industrious, rose early, gave Kate and Johnny a knock, and was out working all day.

The rest of the house's accommodation was occupied by Mr and Mrs Denton and their small child. A good deal older than his wife, he was the type of *rentier* perhaps even then dying out. He was plainly able to afford the price of a furnished flat, a lavish supply of gin, and a habit of eating out. He seemed to have no occupation or hobby beyond this odd version of family life, though procuring sufficient gin in those austere days may have passed much of his time. Boozing led to detectable marital disharmony, or *vice versa* – voices and sounds heard from behind closed doors, tappings on which and pleas to be admitted sometimes taking place in the night. When, more than twenty-five years later I wanted in *The Carnal Island* to suggest marriage's hidden strangeness I remembered the Dentons' bedroom door.

Mrs Slate may have had some sort of job – she would have made a good barmaid in the rougher sort of pub – but Mrs Rosewell simply lived on the income from her house, as though it were an oil-well. A good part of her mornings was occupied with studying the runners and riders, and preparing her betting slip for the day, items of which might be as modest as a sixpenny treble. I came as much as I did into the life of the house – a life suitable for depiction in one of those stage sets where the removal of an exterior wall reveals incongruous though occasionally related activity – because now I was commissioned I usually found it possible to get away from *Ariel* early on Saturday and return on Sunday evening. The manoeuvre was illegal, for sleeping out was not permitted, but of course no pass or watch-card was demanded of officers at the gate, so it was simply a question of walking in and out. The ostensible innocence of that operation I maintained by keeping a set of shaving things, pyjamas, and the like, at the flat, and going through the gate simply with a book under my arm. The latter part of Saturday morning instruction conveniently consisted of an inspection of the radio and radar actually installed in various specimen aircraft ranged round the parade ground, the demonstrator a mere N.C.O. Tearing myself from the spectacle of black-stockinged Wren legs, revealed by the necessary scrambling in and out of the crates, I would walk purposefully away from the group, as though taken short or keeping an appointment with the Chief Writer about income tax. Success made my departure get more brazenly early. But one is inclined to forget the toil and anxiety attending wartime journeyings. A bus had to be caught into Warrington, other military establishments fortunately farther down the road – the full bus passing disconsolate airmen. The fast train to Blackpool usually meant standing in the corridor; the slow train was abyssmally slow, I believe involved a change. Coming back, the Sunday late train missed the last bus; unreliable and much sought after, the taxi that might take one to the camp if one waited long enough outside Warrington's squalid and dimly-lit railway station.

So more often than not I arrived back mid-evening. On one such occasion, walking up the side road to *Ariel* from the bus stop, book under my arm, I could not avoid falling in with the Station Commander. It was late spring or early summer, still light. In my mind I assumed the character of one returning from a local evening saunter, broken by a spell on some grassy bank reading a few pages of Henry James. Like the officer in charge of Seafield Park, the C.O. of *Ariel* was middle-aged, a commissioned warrant officer, now with two-and-a-half stripes. He was shortish, substantially built; the animal with him, likewise. No airs and graces had been assumed by him since his days as gunner or whatever, his naval service probably stretching back to initiation as boy seaman in the *Ganges* of old. Though it does not do to underestimate the regular Navy, it was unlikely he recognized me as an individual, but my still-bright one wavy stripe, with the 'A' in the curl, sufficiently marked me as an officer under instruction. He was walking his dog: so far as known, his pets (unlike those of the Seafield Park C.O.) confined to the canine species. The pace must have been slow, for we passed from generalities to his confiding that he had been suffering from an extremely heavy cold, despite the weather.

'I knew boiled onions and hot whisky would do me good, but there weren't any. So I had a few gins and ate a lot of spring onions. When I went to bed and lay down, the corner of the bed reared up. My God, I thought I was going to be thrown out of it. Never had such an experience . . .'

There is a temptation to depict him as a Lancastrian, have him say 'By Gum' not 'My God' and, like my grandfather, use the word 'scallion' for spring onion, but I forget what the accent was, if identifiable. Certainly the boiled onions remedy smacked of the North, was not unknown to me, so I was able to add to the topic, particularly being already suspicious of gin, giving up the tipple for good after the war when my duodenal ulcer was x-rayed. My enthusiasm for the discussion would not be decreased by a nervous concern to avoid attention to my own recent pursuits, though I cannot recall whether the gin and scallions therapy had actually worked.

One morning at breakfast time – it must have been 7 June 1944 – I heard the wireless in the anteroom speaking of successful Allied landings in Normandy. It was the long-awaited Second Front, thought by some, probably including me, to have been delayed unduly while Uncle Joe consumed his men and *matériel*. Did one feel guilty that the end of the war in Europe was apparently going to come while one putted at weekends in Happy Valley? Perhaps the *Ariel* course itself, interminable, a real grind, provided any absolution required. Against security regulations, I retained on demobilization a 'Sketch Book', so called by the Stationery Office, one of a number used up during the course – a substantial notebook, broader than long, notes on the plain pages, circuit-diagrams and the like on the facing graph pages. I suppose I thought I might one day want to distil it for literary purposes, which indeed I did for the brief lovers' dialogue about the radio altimeter in *The Perfect Fool*. The sketch book contains descriptions, and setting-up and servicing instructions for much ordinary radio equipment. As has been seen, I never had anything to do with such equipment as a rating, and on the course found it boring in content and confusing in multiplicity. How could any officer hope to be usefully familiar with its whole range? His practical role would be to consult his notes or the instruction manual should his specialist subordinates ever be up a gum tree. Nevertheless, I see my notes and drawings are surprisingly clear and neat, and of course I had to pass tests on the sets. Radar interested me much more, appealing to the side of my mind that apart from some layman's reading in various sciences had been unexercised since, as sufficiently bragged about in an earlier volume, I left Seafolde House with distinctions in matriculation Mathematics and Additional Mathematics.

In the second part of his autobiography, *I Am My Brother*, John Lehmann says I returned from East Africa 'indefinably suggesting that some inspirational ghost of himself had been left behind.' Though it does not do to discount anything said by him about human beings, I never took that remark seriously until this moment, when I wonder why I failed to write anything, or anything that has survived, during that *Ariel* time. However, I must immediately add that however solipsistic these writings make me out to be, I have always considered generalities about one's spiritual state from time to time of little validity, most epochs of one's life requiring one simply to soldier on, anything less landing one in a state utterly foreign to one's being. As to the passage of the many *Ariel* weeks, some account could be constructed by taking thought, but in unprompted memory they are curiously neutral and blank. Most evenings in camp I played bridge, always with the same partner, in civilian life a builder from Macclesfield: short, broad, bespectacled, pipe-smoking. We got on well, but he drew atrocious cards with a regularity that smacked of the paranormal, and we were usually a few shillings down the Swanee; rather like being disconcertingly on the wrong end of the solo school on the voyage from Mombasa. Afterwards, bad sleep – not through worry about bridge losses but the result of several psychosomatic factors, actual or incipient ailments already overmuch dwelt on in these memoirs. In my mind's eye I see through my cabin window the dawn coming up beyond the more or less featureless South Lancashire plain.

Jack Beeching – poet, novelist, historian, Petty Officer – claims to have visited me in my cabin at that epoch, but only by pure imagination do I remember the occasion. We met again after the war and despite his living abroad have kept up a friendship. Why I have not asked him if he retains any non-imaginative details of me at *Ariel* is a question perhaps characteristic of those raised by this narrative in the reflective mind. I went once, to play a few rubbers of bridge, into my young brother-in-law's mess of sprogs, taking off my cap at the entrance to indicate an informal visit; gesture doubtless inculcated by my recent *alma mater*, St. John's School, though possibly archetypal, stemming from serials in *Chums* or the *B.O.P.* Colin told my wife he was greatly impressed by my authoritarian bearing and command at morning Divisions. That provides another glimpse into the *Ariel* emptiness, though since the role was confined to calling a Division to attention and reporting it to the Officer of the Day, the encomium was modest – unless arising from an occasion when I *was* O.O.D., a slightly larger part.

The course closed with written and practical examinations, the latter puzzling not only to me. Peter Lavender told of his great fortune in finding an imposed *recherché* fault: 'I just prodded about with a screwdriver and a piece of wire came up "boing!"' Soon after, an officer arrived from the Admiralty to interview us about appointments. A first and second choice could be expressed. As so often in the war, I was dead lucky: my first horse, the Admiralty, came home; my alternative, a British-based carrier, never ran – though I think London had already the disadvantage of raids by V-1s, the pilotless jets. With me, when I took up residence in the Paddington Grande Hotel, was the other Admiralty appointee, the Macclesfield builder.

The hotel was in the purlieus of Praed Street, as indicated by the first and only strictly accurate part of its name. I cannot remember the address, nor could I lead anyone to the spot, and the hotel may well have been redeveloped, for no such name appears in the current telephone directory. How we came to choose it is as mysterious as its location. One would have thought arriving from the north, and with my Gibson & Weldon days, we would have fixed on Bloomsbury, also more convenient for Lower Regent Street (we were not assigned to the Admiralty building proper), but some unknown force had drawn us to W.2., and to an establishment whose general unsatisfactoriness is exemplified in my memory by American military personnel late at night in the corridors, and a condom floating in a lavatory pan. The Macclesfield builder departed swiftly, finding some serviceman's hostel. (Indeed, he also hated the appointment; soon engineered his return to *Ariel*, where he took charge of a specialist mobile repair unit to which my brother-in-law was eventually drafted, in the incestuous manner of Fleet Air Arm encounters.)

Yet even as I write the foregoing paragraph another memory, prompted by the phrase 'some serviceman's hostel', comes vividly to mind – a window open in the summer night looking out over the umbrageousness of Green Park, a high window of Piccadilly premises taken over for the duration as an officers' club, where it was possible to stay quite cheaply for a maximum of a couple of days. It may have been that I had come there from post-course leave in Blackpool, and that the Paddington Grande Hotel advertised its attractions, with other such places, on the noticeboard. Against this version of history is that I was seemingly not with the Macclesfield builder.

For at the officers' club, bedrooms were shared, and when I went alone to mine in the early evening I saw that the other bed was in use, occupation being most strikingly evidenced by the books on the bedside locker, which included *Penguin New Writing* and more esoteric items of contemporary literature I cannot now put a name to. Some spare clothing or perhaps a mere green suitcase indicated that my fellow occupant was in the Navy, and I actually divined in a matter of moments who he must be, so rigorous were the sieves of literary sophistication and the Andrew. We came in at different times to settle down and sleep, so did not speak until the morning. Typically, I failed to let on that I had guessed his identity until sufficient conversation had elapsed about the things that concerned us both – good poetry, good poets and, with equal discrimination, bad ditto.

My vis-à-vis was then just twenty-two. I suppose in those days one knew the name, had made an assessment, of every contributor to approved (and, indeed, disapproved) magazines, but at that moment there must have been little work of Alan Ross to go on, perhaps only a few poems in *P.N.W.* I am sure he did not appear in any O.K. mental list of mine. I probably thought that as well as having still to prove himself he might be, as a member of the next (or even next but one) generation of poets, infected by Neo-Romanticism – to use an omnibus term for all new poetry that disobeyed Geoffrey Grigson's Thirties summation of 1939, and failed to take 'notice, for ends not purely individual, of the universe

118

of objects and events.' I expect I was to a degree guarded in those preliminary exchanges above Piccadilly, little envisaging the long years of friendship that followed, down to this day. Alan Ross, however romantic his appearance and beginnings, soon showed himself as someone who made me laugh; wise in judgements; staunch in loyalties; and who followed Sassoon's dictum to 'sweat your guts out' writing poetry.

I wonder if even in Paddington Grande Hotel days I had not already met, either at that first Lehmann party or through J. R. Ackerley, William Plomer, for I moved from the hotel's sleaziness to accommodation not strikingly better in Linden Gardens (now apparently called Linden Mews) off the Bayswater Road. William lived either in that square or the next, and it seems too much of a coincidence that I should have chosen the district, hitherto unknown, utterly at random. My room, though pleasantly overlooking the Square garden, was hamperingly narrow, formed from a larger room by a partition that admitted dubious sounds; furnishing, ambience and denizens of the quarter reminiscent of my Bloomsbury digs of more than a decade earlier, and which would have offended my mother's keen liking for cleanliness, respectability and comfort scarcely the less. No meals were supplied, so I usually called at Lyons' Coventry Street 'Corner House' for breakfast before proceeding to Lower Regent Street.

I can still summon up the atmosphere in 1944 of the ground-floor restaurant, the only part of the large, multi-floored establishment serving breakfasts, but who can it interest save the relatively few surviving customers of those years? – a substantial number of the population being now with dim notions, or none, of what a Corner House was. One passed through the shopping foyer (the stalls of bread, chocolates, and the like, not yet stocked and open for business) to the restaurant at the rear, windowless and thus always in artificial light, 'orange-rosy lamps' (to use Arthur Symons's phrase), an affair of marble and mahogany veneers. There was usually some anxiety about securing a place at one of the many small tables, war-time shortage of *maîtres-d'hôtel* allowing separate pockets of waiting customers and queue-jumping, perhaps other anarchies. A similar feeling-tone attached itself to ordering from the hard-worked waitresses – as to when the previous breakfaster's debris would be cleared, not mistaken for one's own; what might remain available on the menu, and so forth. The tension pending the actual arrival of the food and beverage was not really alleviated

119

by the exiguous morning newspaper, already sucked fairly dry on the way. Bacon and tomato comes to mind as one of the superior dishes, not always available. The portion of preserve allotted failed adequately to cover what was left of one's two slices of faintly buttered toast after the main dish had been consumed. Because of one's uniform, favoured treatment seemed to come from the waitresses (the eternal feminine throbbing under their black and white garb), but in what this resided is now difficult to specify. Further anxiety about waiting for the bill was avoided by asking for it when the order was delivered. By the time one emerged, the shop stalls were in business, and could be scanned for any rare delicacy available, either on or off rationing 'points' or coupons.

Rex House, my destination in Lower Regent Street, was a modern office building partly taken over to house Admiralty departments. The Directorate of Naval Air Radio (D.N.A.R.) was where *Ariel*-trained Admiralty appointees normally went, but my appointment was to the Directorate of Air Equipment (D.A.E.), the logic being to have someone there who could see that a naval aircraft's other equipment harmonized with its radio and radar sets, and also to look after items to do with radio and radar whose supply and fitting were the responsibility of D.A.E. rather than D.N.A.R. I was in a not-large room with four other officers, initially five, for I had a brief overlapping period with the officer I was to succeed. We sat at tables, three facing three, nearness to the window depending on seniority. Diagonally opposite me, by the window, only partly visible behind accumulated files, volumes of Admiralty Fleet Orders (A.F.O.s) and other technical works, sat Cornish-Bowden, a Commander in the Supply Branch. Above a dark-eyed, sallow face, his thin black hair was brilliantined close to his head. I would sometimes out of earshot refer to him as Cornish-Pasty, the puerile vulgarism not unapt having regard to his complexion. Of all the room's occupants it was he who took things most seriously, writing as relentlessly as Sir Walter Scott, calling subordinates over the coals, not infrequently going next door to confer with the Director. One saw that for him the Admiralty appointment was a vital stage in his career, next job, promotion even, dependent on his performance. When I first joined D.A.E. the man on his left was also regular Navy, a Commander with pilot's wings – good-looking, with the traditional slightly too-posh but attractive, naval officer's accent. He was my immediate superior; once asked me to go to the Hungaria restaurant a few doors away and book a table for two for supper, which I did – the morning ambience of a smart place where one danced between courses so strange that I noted it as a possible background in future fiction.

The officer opposite Cornish-Bowden has virtually gone from memory. Next to me was a tall, thin R.N.R. officer wearing the general service ribbons of the First War – except for that indication, of indeterminate age. Though perfectly agreeable, he was unforthcoming to all and sundry, occupying himself, in a way that always seemed difficult to account for, with but a single category of equipment – though that, admittedly, expensive and complicated: Link Trainers. It was a job he was said to have had since the start of the War. At first, in my ignorance, I thought 'Link' stood for some continuing process in the training of pilots, perhaps in an undefined manner even embracing group psychology, not realising it was the inventor's name. Quite strange that he and others, far from the stereotypes of literature, should have come down the years in sketchable form, not precluding greater depth of depiction.

We all had numbers: E5, the Lieutenant I was to inherit this title from, as in some secret society, sat opposite me for the few days of our ambiguous duplication. E5 was a cheerful, extravert young man, with pilot's wings. It soon appeared he had crashed an aircraft, I think in the course of some ferrying job; perhaps had displayed other less sensational disadvantages for the pilot's profession, and been sent to D.A.E. to be 'lost'. I would have said myself he was less fitted for an office than for the occupation he had just left. One of the first files (or dockets, as perhaps they were known) to arrive from the Registry (the central filing and recording system, staffed by civil servants) concerned the provision of flying helmets for the Fleet Air Arm. It was marked to E5, who (though sequent markings would ensure its passage to the Hungarian Commander and, through Cornish-Bowden, probably to D.A.E. himself) was plainly expected to name a figure. The problem was reminiscent of those tricky ones about water running into cisterns with outlets, encountered at school, but E5 tackled it with the confidence that must have got him his wings. 'Let's put 30,000,' he said, as I momentarily sat next to him, the better to observe his craft.

Memory may have got the figure wrong, but surely it was of that order. At first I imagined that in his noddle E5 had information about the rate of flow, but, on questioning, he never convinced me that more than guesswork was involved. Though the figure seemed to me more appropriate to the R.A.F. than the F.A.A., I weakly allowed the minute to embody it, and the docket to pass on. It is no defence to recall that some of the more commonplace aspects of the appointment still held mystery – the proper form of minutes ('I propose the following minute' was the opening for an underling), meaning of initials and acronyms, whereabouts of liaison officers, departmental sections, other Government and service departments – for having worked in a large organization the pennies quickly dropped. One more-abiding puzzle was the bottle of apparent lighter-fluid among the paper-clips and ashtrays on most officers' desks. With a poet's blend of gormlessness and over-ingenious subtlety (or maybe the mix was merely constitutional), I thought there might be a gin issue to compensate for absence of wardroom facilities, kept by the recipients in a form handy for a quick nip – rather like Pogson and Bridle with superfluous rum. Of course, the bottles proved in truth to contain lighter-fluid, displayed because officers sat not at desks but drawerless tables. The business is reminiscent of a howler I perpetrated in the Third Form at Seafolde House, translating a piece of French prose. The master singled out my translation as the only one in decent English, then pricked any vanity by adding that it contained a curious (his word) error. I had rendered *Il jeta un coup d'oeil sur le voyageur* – 'He threw a cup of oil over the traveller.' The thing seems almost unbelievably ludicrous now, but I know precisely what was in my mind. The context was a journey by stagecoach, and I imagined the oil as a protection from the elements for an outside passenger, rather as channel swimmers are greased before plunging in.

I got a second chance at the flying-helmets problem. Whether the docket was returned by E2 (or whatever the Hungarian officer's number was) or I rescued it when E5 had gone, I do not recall. In any case, because of my own dubieties the question became part of a much larger one; namely, the provision of earphones and microphones to go, as it were, with the flying-helmets. It was a business pretty far removed from any gen acquired at *Ariel*, even such fundamental knowledge needing research as to whether every earphone jack would fit into the relevant radio-set socket. For when one looked at the massive loose-leaf catalogue of Fleet Air Arm stores (borrowed from the barricade round Cornish-Bowden), types of earphones and microphones (and even of flying-helmets) were revealed in considerable number. Which was compatible with which was not specified, nor whether some were merely historical: the conscientious stores officer, in carrier or base, would see he was stocked up with all types, in common use or not. The position was complicated by the then new-fangled throat-microphones. My thrifty temperament, sharpened by the solicitor's training that instils logicality and tidiness of thought, was appalled, and I was drawn into a one-man enquiry as to obsolete, obsolescent and currently-used helmets, earphones and microphones in the F.A.A. Some of this consisted of interrogation of individual officers in D.A.E. For instance, there was the big, jolly, but responsible pilot in the section – perhaps *was* the section – that liaised with Staff in the Admiralty proper. In the fascinating room in D.A.E. whose walls depicted the changing global patterns of F.A.A. squadrons, their whereabouts, aircraft types and numbers, and equipment state, I found Lieutenant Kingsmill, young survivor of the heroic Swordfish attack on the *Scharnhorst* and *Gneisenau*, recovered from his wounds, and witty and intelligent, though plainly still a shadow of his former self: he was another whose microphone lore I listened to.

When, quite recently, I belatedly read the biographical book by R. F. Harrod about Lindemann, *The Prof*, I was greatly pleased to come across the following:

> They [the Fleet Air Arm] had a professional statistician, a highly efficient one as I was to find, Mr R. E. Beard of the Prudential Assurance Company. When asked some question on the telephone, such as how many new propellors were still needed for Swordfish aircraft, he could make calculations from complicated basic data by playing lightly on the calculating machine with one hand while he held the receiver with the other, and give the correct answer almost without any delay.

Plainly, the solution of the problem originally posed to E5 depended on the prognosticated entry to the F.A.A. of aircrew, and their rate of wastage. Someone must surely have a notion of these figures. I made enquiries, I believe of the directorate's civil servants, and was put on to Mr Beard. I went to see him in his modest office: found him broad, blond, youngish, genial; head large, in the manner Wodehouse conceived his brainy characters to be cast. As in Roy Harrod's experience, he seemed quite prepared to give me an answer on the spot, but I think in the end said he would put it on paper. I consulted him a few times on that and other business, reassured to find such a chap involved in the conduct of the war.

It turned out that a number of items of the equipment in question were of a certainty no longer in use; other items needed co-ordinating. That section of the stores book required drastic emendation. I drafted the necessary A.F.O., and even Cornish-Pasty found little wrong with it. I give, of course, a truncated version of the action, for the minute proposing the A.F.O. must have made the rounds of other directorates before their Lordships passed it into law. I have gone on about the matter, low-toned and tedious though most will find it, because it was my greatest contribution to what was commonly called 'the war effort', eclipsing the work with Bob Park in and from the iffy hut.

In my time in D.A.E. there was only one item of radio or radar equipment for which D.A.E. rather than D.N.A.R. was responsible, and which therefore fell to my lot. It had been pretty well fully developed before I arrived, may already have been in process of manufacture. I have tried and failed to recall its code-name, once as familiar as my own. If ever brought to the mind's surface it would probably at once betray its Freudian guiltiness. The item in question was a battery-powered radar beacon that sent out a signal on the A.S.V. frequency. Its components had been 'miniaturized' (term and process still novel at that time) so that it was no larger than a large electric torch, and could be accommodated in an aircrew member's 'Mae West'. If he were forced to ditch he would switch on the beacon and thus indicate his whereabouts on the screen of a rescuing aircraft, enabling it to home on him. The great crux when I came into the story was where the thing could be stowed in the already overcrowded Mae West. One of the competing objects was a bakelite box containing such essentials for survival as boiled sweets and a fishing line. At a joint meeting of departments concerned, some specimens of these boxes were produced by the representative of MI9, and I secured one for my son's amusement, risking a foreign agent seeing him playing with it in Mrs Rosewell's house. The MI9 man was another character from Wodehouse – Sub-Lieutenant the Lord Holden: slight, with a gingerish beard; could be envisaged clean-shaven in the Drones Club.

In the account thus far of life in an Admiralty department, perhaps too many trivialities have been particularised. Yet writing, I have a constant sense of the insufficiently factual, though working detail in, so to speak, is almost as much an effort of technique as of memory. I spent some months in D.A.E. Among a few oddly-surviving papers, come across of late, are two quarterly pay statements from the department, running to 31 March 1945, but I believe I may have moved from the department physically if not administratively before that date. (With pay and various allowances, my emoluments as a sub-lieutenant were getting on for £700 a year, giving substance to the jest I made in a speech on some Woolwich Equitable occasion after the war, that in the end far from the Society making up my salary I was paying them; a dig appreciated by those whose salaries had been frozen while on National Service, and never thoroughly thawed out.) Every day at Rex House a mass of incident must be envisaged, much of it of a period character. There was the appearance of a Parker 51 in the hands of an officer who had served in or visited the United States, the first time a fountain-pen nib had been hooded, the cap-retention device on the barrel also surely novel in giving an almost perfectly smooth grip. Such an implement seemed one of the most desirable possessions in the world, but I was not able to buy one until on holiday in Switzerland in 1947. There was an attractive young woman in the Registry, and who therefore came round the offices with dockets, referred to on one occasion as 'the Sweater Girl' by none other than Cornish-Bowden, who may have been previously depicted with too sombre a palette. The name stuck but struck me as unapt, for though a sweater was almost always on view it was massively occupied, and for me the cognomen demanded more subtlety, as in the case of Lana Turner, I believe its original possessor.

There were the perennial problems of eating, over and above the breakfasts already lingered over. In the basement of Rex House was an odorous canteen, cafeteria style, not much used by me, reminiscent of the British Restaurant, phenomenon of the times, touched on in *Vamp*. Higher up the street, in what is now the Ceylon Tea Centre, was the Canadian Officers' Club, not really a club nor restricted to Canadians, consequently always crowded, the food as I recall it quite passable, slightly transatlantic. Once a week, perhaps more frequently, I lunched with J. R. Ackerley and William Plomer at Shearn's, the vegetarian shop and restaurant in Tottenham Court Road, now no more. Nut rissole with a thick brown gravy, and syrup-sponge pudding, is the sort of menu that sticks in the memory (as doubtless it stuck in my digestive tracts), though salads must also have been on offer. I had got to know Joe Ackerley through sending poems to *The Listener*, of which he was literary editor. He had taken a poem as early as 1940, but I did not meet him until 1944. Looking at my file of his letters, which

I assembled when Neville Braybrooke, editing Joe's letters for publication, asked to see them, I note that a letter of 16 December 1943 says he was 'sorry not to be able to come and meet you at Lehmann's the other day.' That more or less dates the Lehmann party and confirms my recollection of first seeing Joe at Broadcasting House.

In reviewing the flurry of books by and concerning Joe of recent years, I have brought in some memories and descriptions of him which I do not feel like repeating here, so will try to say something fresh. It may well be the revelations about his life by himself and others has left a disagreeable impression in many readers' minds, so I ought to emphasise that I liked him a lot, as did my wife, and that apart from making me go a bit red a time or two in those early Shearn days, through his occasional frankness about physical matters, nothing a heterosexual petty bourgeois might find untoward emanated from him. In 1944 he was forty-eight. He was thought extremely handsome as a young man, and some photographs confirm this. In middle-age he wore very ordinary spectacles, and tweed-jacket-grey-slacks sort of clothes, with a beret in inclement weather: these contributed to the lack of distinction that had crept over him, perhaps were its source, for though he merged easily into saloon bar surroundings there was nothing shabby or commonplace about his voice, manner, hands, management of a cigarette. (Lack of distinction is rather too harsh a phrase, any way.) By publishing *Hindoo Holiday* in 1932 he had just about sustained the youthful fame brought by his play *Prisoners of War*, but since then no book by him had appeared. When I met him I had not read *Hindoo Holiday*, though aware of it. Like *Seven Gothic Tales*, its reputation had made it seem a book I would not particularly care for, but when I repaired my omission after getting to know Joe I thought it, as many did, a classic, an opinion I have had no reason to change.

At the Admiralty I had only one or two little poems to let Joe look at for *The Listener*, but I see from the old cuttings-book, previously consulted, that I began reviewing for him in September 1944, provoking kerfuffles almost immediately. *Listener* reviewing was then anonymous, so obloquy tended to be piled on the Literary Editor by any of the reviewed who were offended, unable otherwise to syphon off their wrath. Joe asked me to review Edith Sitwell's *Green Song and Other Poems*, which foolishly I did. I believe my original notice was quite short and that Joe suggested I extend it by including more illustrative quotation. Considering the *Listener*'s limited space, the result was an ample review, and I see in it evidence of what I have rarely done as a reviewer, that is to lean backwards to perceive virtue, and to have some regard for the paper's position in relation to the author. Briefly, my thesis was that Edith Sitwell had made a great effort to rise to the poetic demands of the war after 'a life-time's verse which can hardly be said to be other than minor verse of a limited kind', but that judging *Green Songs* by the highest standards its imagery 'is for the most part monotonous and unclear, and of very unequal significance.' No need to go on: some words of praise do not affect the firm thumbs-down for the notion, then being canvassed, that Edith Sitwell's war-time verse was of Yeatsian calibre.

It may be thought there was not much pulling of punches in these remarks, but my inclination was to be a good deal sharper, convinced that Edith Sitwell's reputation was growing out of hand and ought to be slashed. (Oddly enough, today I would want to be more generous to the pre-war verse, for its fantasy and original technique has weathered well.) Publishing the review, it was said, got Joe struck off the list of house-guests for Renishaw Hall, the Sitwell country mansion. I knew from him that Edith was outraged but he never disclosed the extent of the sanctions imposed, nor did he utter a word of complaint. Indeed, six weeks later he printed a review of mine of *New Writing and Daylight* in which I said that an Edith Sitwell essay about the Greek poet and critic Demetrios Capetanakis, recently dead at a tragically early age, was 'quite remarkable for its overstatement, and rather predisposes one against' the other essays on Capetanakis. These included pieces by William Plomer and John Lehmann. The publication of this second review was, according to Victoria Glendinning's biography of Edith Sitwell, one of the causes of her writing to John Lehmann: 'The dregs of the literary population have risen as one worm to insult me.' Capetanakis had been a close friend of John Lehmann (and Edith Sitwell was, to a degree) so I thought it right to tell John I was the author of words that might rankle with him, especially if not carefully read. He was very cross; I righteous but perturbed: we were estranged for some months – the only such episode in a friendship as old as my son; forty-six years, as I write these words.

I do not think Edith Sitwell herself was aware of the perpetrator of these heinous crimes, for I feel sure it was later I was presented to her at a Lehmann party and exchanged courtesies, the occasion (already a *leitmotiv* in my memoirs) when her likeness to Max

127

Miller was pointed out to me by William Plomer. William, at the era of the Shearn's lunches, was also in the Admiralty, a temporary civil servant in some intelligence department, possibly Sub-Lieut-enant the Lord Holden's. I liked William but never knew him well. He had by this date effected the change from dissident colonial to Establishment man of letters noted by Laurens van der Post in his recent book *Yet Being Someone Other*, describing it as effected 'with conscious determination and against the stream of natural instincts'. William and Joe and John Morris were reported in the stalls of the Camberwell Green Empire at a travelling revue of the day, *Soldiers in Skirts*, but this may possibly have been a joke and in any event does not much detract from the sober and respectable persona William presented – English accent, voice sensationally deep; hair neatly *en brosse*; spectacles and tweed jacket and flannel trousers, a nuttier version of Joe's.

Thinking about these matters, it strikes me what a dull dog I must have been at the Shearn's lunches, not able to contribute much to the gossip about people, nor educe anything amusing from my own life. It would never have occurred to me to go on about Mrs Slate, say, though both William and Joe had a great interest in the nominally ordinary. I cannot say I was awed: simply by tempera-ment and rearing unable to summon up the light garrulity known as 'small talk', though I daresay I more than held my own with friends like Willie Robertson and Jack Jolly; trait I have touched on before. No, I was not awed, but the Sleuthing Aldous Huxley syndrome (see *Vamp*) still to a degree persisted: it was a notable occasion for me when John and Myfanwy Piper joined us at Shearn's: he with premature white hair and bright blue shirt, she with uncurled hair and no make-up – a respectable Bohemianism that part of my apprehension might well have been storing away for unflattering use. I admit to being awed when the party joining us was E. M. Forster (the venue being changed to the Akropolis or perhaps the White Tower, Percy Street restaurants), but again what enured was the incongruous, the potentially comic – the eminent novelist's brown-suited insignificance, inclining to the shabby. I used elements of the occasion more than twenty-five years later for the first meeting of the old and young poets in my novel *The Carnal Island*.

Shearn's cuisine and the missile of the time came together in William's poem 'The Flying Bum: 1944', in which a V-1 or 'flying bomb' explodes outside a vegetarian guest-house and deposits a 'lightly roasted rump of horse' on a dining-table previously occupied only by 'imitation sausage/Made of monkey-nuts and spice.' The question never arose of our meeting in or near Linden Gardens; nor, though he gave me the telephone number, did I ever visit Joe's Putney flat, its curiously squalid romanticism now public property through various Ackerleyiana. It was less being sexually not 'of their kind' that confined our friendship than my lack of push and (I guess) their domestic constrictions.

Laurie Lee could well have been the informant about intellectual elements in the South London audience for *Soldiers in Skirts*. I used to see quite a bit of him, despite the attention diverted from *A Lost Season* by his *The Sun my Monument*. Though at this epoch the war-time job already mentioned provided a decent reason or excuse, he had already perfected the strategy that served him well during the ensuing peace: that is, enhancing his reputation with a severely limited production, parsimony some other literary figures one might name could better have copied. In those early days he actually passed on to me an assignment that had come his way – to write the commentary for a pictorial history of the war thus far. The pictures were to be shown on a screen of modest size, sections lighting up automatically as the relevant stage of the recorded spoken commentary was reached. The assignment came from the Hungarian refugee inventor of this device, which was to stand and do its stuff in Ford's motor-car showrooms, then next to or near the Café Royal in Regent Street. The fee offered was £50, substantial for the time, and I felt I could not turn it down. It was my first experience of something foolishly or weakly repeated down to this day – undertaking literary work at the behest and under the control of others, always laborious and jejune in the composition, usually unsatisfactory in the result, sometimes shamefully tinged with falsity. For many years now my motivation has been not money but friendship or too great a concern for the entrepreneurial problems of others, even strangers; curious twist of character. As to the chore Laurie typically attracted and wisely avoided, in due course I stepped up from Rex House one lunchtime and heard (with needless embarrassment, for my part was anonymous) the machine speaking my lines. I expect they were disappointingly unpatriotic, non-Churchillian; nevertheless far from the Marxist dubieties of my real views.

When I first knew Laurie I thought his Gloucestershire accent Canadian; the kind of misconception age has not entirely eradi-

129

cated. I daresay our friendship was helped by congenial encounters at parties or poetry-readings, though if asked to specify them I would be gravelled. In fact, the only poetry-reading of the time I can recall was a quite grand affair, for charity, including Laurie but also C. Day Lewis and Louis MacNeice. Afterwards, Anthony Panting, an active photographer in those days, known through Jack Clark, said my contribution was unlike the rest, an observation that has stuck in my mind. No doubt being the only performer in uniform (*Soldiers in Skirts* in reverse, so to speak) was a sufficient differentiation, but I think Anthony was referring, approvingly, to the generally non-poetic or non-conventionally-poetic in my performance and material. I expect I read then, as I do now, for sense; hoping not to falter over the rhythm but certainly not adopting a sing-song or incantatory manner. When I hear on the wireless a snatch of Dylan Thomas reading his verse I am amazed the business is still taken seriously, so outrageous, even risible, an example is it of pre-war theatrical hamming. Readers of *Souvenirs* may remember the silver-locked, velvet-coated elocutionist Rider Boys, temporary visiting staff member at Seafolde House: he recited with the tongue of a Thomas.

And what parties could I have attended in uniform, except John Lehmann's? It may have been just after rather than during the war that I got to know Rose Macaulay well enough to go up to her at such gatherings, at which she was an assiduous attender. Only my Aldous Huxley syndrome prompted me to do it, for I had never read her novels, and though she was always forthcoming in her rapid Bloomsbury voice, chewed by her front teeth (almost as marked in her deathshead as in an actual skull), we had little or no shared experience. But a few of her verses had been in one of the *Poems of Today* anthologies, a set book for the Oxford Junior or School Certificate examination I had sat at Seafolde House. Even then I could have quoted from 'Many Sisters to Many Brothers', a patriotic poem of hers from the First World War. At the epoch of the Second War and thereafter, her physique resembled that of a startlingly emaciated family friend of my schooldays, who according to my mother had to eat raw liver to keep pernicious anaemia at bay. My slight courting of Rose Macaulay shows there still burned the curious desire for literary fame that had arisen, without apparent ancestry, quite early on at Seafolde House.

I was still in D.A.E. when I started *Savage Gold*, 'a story of adventure', as it was eventually subtitled. A picture coheres of writing it in the same sort of Stationery Office notebook as contained the brief journal previously quoted, sitting on the Cornish-Bowden side of the row of tables for some reason – perhaps during the evening of a duty officer night, a chore that occasionally came round, involving sleeping on the duty officer's bed, keeping an eye on the signals in the signals room, sometimes (as at Tanga) wandering about in search of reading matter if one had miscalculated, in the former tradition of E2, requirements in that line. One thinks now that one would not have dared to work on the thing in office hours, but who knows what schoolboyish masks of blotting-paper and dockets might not have been brought into play, even within sight of Cornish-Bowden? The *genre* aimed at in *Savage Gold* was roughly that of *Treasure Island*. Quite apart from the motive of trying to entertain my son, I felt my fictive powers were not up to the adult novel. That conviction was due less to the past history of novels abandoned, and the novel completed but never published, than to a sense that my invention could not engage the mature reader. I was still hung-over with technical problems from the past. I did not want to enter and stay imprisoned *à la* Dalloway in some single consciousness, yet saw no way of escaping except through the juvenile tale of action or the whodunnit, a form I came to immediately after *Savage Gold*. I think even as I embarked on *Savage Gold* I envisaged gradually easing myself into fully-felt, and technically flexible, adult fiction. I fear I have touched on this theme before, not least the irony that though in the end my novels would have satisfied many of my schoolboy day-dreams thereof, they are now virtually out of print, rapidly becoming forgotten as their original readers die off.

How steeped one had been as an adolescent in the Joycean or Woolfian interior style was shown by the ludicrous difficulty I had, getting going with *Savage Gold*, of straightforwardly describing events. At some early stage I recalled Flaubert's employment of brief, purely factual sentences at critical moments: Hemingway also uses the device. Bathetic and naive to say so, but I followed them. Though I set the story in the Africa I knew, I imported into it elements of the world the great African explorers found towards the end of the nineteenth century, so that the book must read oddly in the times of Oboto and Mugabwe. On the other hand, the essential character of some present-day régimes is not too far from that of the kingdom of the Wazamba in *Savage Gold*. Perhaps the years will eventually smooth down historical discrepancies, and a few boys read its yellowing pages as gospel.

It was one of the first publications of the firm founded by John Lehmann on his break from the Hogarth Press in 1946. Brilliantly illustrated by Robert Medley (designer for Rupert Doone's Group Theatre and an inspired choice of John Lehmann's), it proved my most successful book, appearing before books lost their war-time scarcity and saleability. Later, Puffin Books did it in paperback; and in 1960 there was a new hardback edition by Hutchinson Educational, aimed at schools. I used to say it would keep me in fags in my old age, but fortunately I gave up smoking at the age of sixty-two.

10.   D.N.A.R.

'My first movement . . . must . . . be in the direction of Blackheath.'

– Conan Doyle: 'The Adventure of the Norwood Builder'

A few weeks ago, quite by chance, I read Angela Thirkell's slight but charmingly accurate autobiographical volume, *Three Houses*, first published in 1931. In it, she refers to her childish practice (of which my Uncle Freddy, devoted sandwich-maker in his youth – have I not written somewhere of his actually contriving sandwiches out of his helping of potato pie? – would have approved) of making a cake sandwich – a slice of cake between slices of bread. That brought back to me the Peele sisters, friends of my East Lancashire boyhood, introducing me to cream cracker sandwiches – a cream cracker between a folded slice of bread-and-butter, preferably brown. I felt sure this was mentioned somewhere in these volumes of memoirs, but have failed to find the reference. No wonder, it may be thought, in an indexless, chronology-defying work. But the thematic return, sometimes in original form, sometimes varied, sometimes seeming new simply through intervening development, is as characteristic of life as of music. And I say 'the Peele sisters', but the cream cracker sandwich was an invention of the elder (it must be added to the sketch of her in *Souvenirs*), who went on, as I heard from afar, to be a doctor. Her gentle character would serve humanity well in that profession; as would her reassuring appearance, which perhaps through years of changing coiffures retained the long hair of her girlhood.

As the Allied invasion of Europe prospered in the summer of 1944, I began to think about *après la guerre*, at least in terms of somewhere to live. It may be that returning to my pre-call-up job as assistant solicitor to the Woolwich Equitable was still a slightly open question, but prudence and convenience indicated a flat in Blackheath, within two or three miles of Woolwich, and locale of our maisonette the landmine wrecked in the Blitz. Plainly, there would be an accommodation famine when the war was over. Nevertheless, an element of daring resided in taking on even a short lease of a flat at what seemed a substantial rent of £2.15s a week. The Admiralty appointment could by no means be considered a permanency, and any move would almost certainly be towards the Far East, Japan looking like long outlasting Germany.

Journeying to Blackheath, nineteen minutes from Charing Cross, by what was still the Southern Railway, to visit estate agents, resembled biting into a cream cracker sandwich. The Village (so called) seemed strange, like some childhood haunt, but of course not so strange as in 1938 when we were scouting out the ground for the move from Ashford. I needed only to consult one firm of agents, Dyer, Son & Creasey (somewhat Dickensian name, still extant), quickly settling on the ground-floor flat in a well-converted, mid-nineteenth century, grey-brick house in a quiet tree-lined road of such, called St. John's Park. This time I did not make the mistake of choosing a side of the heath remote from Woolwich, again rather confirming acceptance of a return to the law. Somewhat later, I was invited to stay on as a regular officer in the Navy, further promotion dangled before me, but surely I could never have seriously considered this – though my brother accepted a similar offer from the R.A.F., an epoch in his life of strange encounters, as touched on in *Souvenirs*. The only change more than fleetingly contemplated was an occupation in Grub Street that would at once have been more congenial than solicitoring and given me greater time to write prose fiction. But the conviction, so strong in the earlier part of the war, among the air-raids and on the lower-deck, that one's life and self would never again be the same, must by now have ceased to grip. Being at the Admiralty was a novitiate to prepare one for a renewal of strict office life – though further service in a far-flung, even dangerous and rowdy parish was by no means ruled out.

The St. John's Park flat consisted of a large sitting-room overlooking a commodious neglected garden, mostly grass; two bedrooms, one enormous, with great mahogany mantelpiece and surround, probably the house's dining-room; and, made out of the former billiards-room annexe, a dining-room and kitchen, reached by a spacious corridor lit by two arched windows and glass double-doors giving on to a conservatory. The solid side of the conservatory had a floor to ceiling rockery down which it had originally been arranged that water should trickle. As a matter of fact, a cress-like growth still flourished there, sustained by rain, for bombing of various kinds had breached the conservatory's defences. It was the rockery feature that led us to nickname the conservatory the 'Reptile House', though the floor of ornamented terra-cotta tiles (reminding me of the floor of the Tanga hospital, which I had traversed to reach this further point in life) contributed to the zoolike atmosphere. The garden could be reached from both kitchen and Reptile House, in the latter case via a quite elegant iron staircase. In a garden a few doors away Charles Peace had been apprehended in 1878, after wounding P.C. Robinson.

The house was owned by a Mrs Hipkin, who lived with her unmarried adult daughter in Bexleyheath. The rents from the four flats were perhaps the major part of their income. At any rate, my being a naval officer and peacetime solicitor proved insufficient credentials, and through the agents an appointment was made for me to meet Mrs and Miss Hipkin on the premises. Did some pieces of furniture or packing-cases linger from the previous tenancy, or did we all stand up during the interview? I clearly recall it taking place in the south-facing sitting-room, light filtering through a species of translucent paper often tacked up at blasted windows by war damage repair contractors in lieu of glass. Discussion ensued about my plans, my family: eventually I was accepted.

An unwritten term of the lease was that I should employ the charlady, Mrs Morris, who had served the former tenant and currently served another tenant in the house. How many mornings a week she was to come to me I forget, but the hourly rate of her three-hour stint was one and fourpence (7p), so on her days on I used to leave a couple of florins (with any Pickwickian message thereunder), for I had departed for Rex House before she arrived. She had a key to let herself in: her utter trustworthiness had been emphasised by the Hipkins. Small, thin, sallow, mildly depressed, limp hats, Chaplinesque feet, she could have played a charlady on the boards – of the effacing kind, though on one topic, her loved daughter, she was dominating in conversation. Occasionally, a day off of mine (perhaps to make up for a Duty Officer night) might coincide with a morning on of hers, and then her maternal monologue would be resumed. But in general our Box and Cox existence was satisfactory. She was a dedicated tidier-up, which was primarily the service I wanted in my initially grass-widowered period. Thoroughness in cleaning was not her *métier*: traces of old food in pans or between tines draw forth even today family accusations of a 'Morrisian' washing-up. Nevertheless, she went on working for us after the war, and for Kathleen and Julian Symons when they eventually came to live in the top flat. Nor was she a great innovator with language, like Proust's Françoise: nothing much in that line has come down, though she did once observe to Kate that 'Mrs Symons's Hoover's an Electrolux.'

Strange epoch, living by myself at 16 St. John's Park; strangeness inaugurated by reception of our goods and chattels from their place of storage. That was another cream-cracker-sandwichlike episode; items miraculously reincarnated, from what seemed a distant past – a few, like a large blue-painted bookcase made by a friend, a neighbouring joiner, recalling Ashford rather than former Blackheath days. In such feelings resided the strangeness; more than the incongruity of, say, establishing permanent relations between my weekly ration card and a local butcher while the final war scenes, with various prolongations and *coups de théâtre*, were being enacted in Europe. That one's life had been disturbed and disrupted, sufficiently countered guilt at one's own piddling activities; besides one was under fire from V weapons.

I must have moved from Bayswater to Blackheath in the not too advanced autumn of 1944, for good weather attended the early days and, looking back, the constriction and comparative squalor of life in Linden Gardens do not seem of awfully long duration. The move preceded my leaving D.A.E. for D.N.A.R. Topographically, the latter shift merely involved another floor of Rex House: essentially, it was a promotion, though my second stripe did not arrive immediately. I became Technical Assistant to the Director of Naval Air Radio, sharing a roomy outer office, protecting the Director's own office, with a Wren secretary. The window at the rear of Rex House, that even Commander Cornish-Bowden had no view from, was exchanged for an interesting panorama of Lower Regent Street.

The Director was Basil Willett who it was said had retired with the rank of Commander before the war, had been brought back with an extra stripe or acquiring one on the way. Presumably he had no detailed knowledge of aircraft radar and radio such as was imparted at *Ariel*; hence the post of Technical Assistant. He was about fifty: a blue-eyed, slightly weather-beaten countenance, what might be romantically thought of as a true sailor's; and with the characteristic naval officer's accent already noted. Behind him was a solid upper middle-class background: he was a son of 'Daylight Saving' Willett, the builder. Once, when I had occasion to speak on the telephone to his home or perhaps his family home, a female retainer referred to him as 'Master Basil'. His enormous 'progress' meetings were famous: I had attended some of them in my role as Mae West beacon king. Now, part of my job was to sit at his side on such occasions, though he betrayed no weakness in technical grasp or, for that matter, any other kind. In fact, he was extremely able and, though capable of fearless strength, exercised his will through completely unselfconscious charm. The accent belonged to a voice slightly hoarse, as though formed in the days when signals were bawled through the tempest. Somewhere in his smile was a hint of gold. He made a good few jokes, usually about the deficiencies of the bodies involved in his meetings, and the recurring personality traits of those representing them. He was a devoted pipe-smoker, getting rid of ash and dottle by inclining his hand, palm up, over an ashtray and knocking the pipe-bowl on his signet-ring. Soon, our intimacy was marked by his calling me 'old' Fuller (I was thirty-two, moustacheless state knocking off a few years in appearance), the adjective as he pronounced it almost a mere 'o'. I write 'intimacy', but I cannot recall my attitude being other than utterly correct. Did I make jokes myself? Impossible now to say.

A tremendous amount of paper came into the Director's office: dockets for his attention, and appreciations, studies and periodicals of diverse kind, many only marginally connected with naval aircraft radar and radio, some from the United States, some Secret and Most Secret, most Confidential. I flatter myself that getting through this stuff, and selecting and presenting the few nuggets I thought Captain Willett should see, was a task up my street. I was a rapid reader, used to dry and complicated prose, soon became familiar with the sources and nature of the bumf, and kept it in subjection. I suppose I must have drafted or suggested minutes, but that side of things has quite faded. It was a revelation to me that some merely technical information was marked as not disclosable to the Soviet Union, though possibly useful against the Germans. That struck me as unfair to an ally who had suffered so much from the enemy. I am sure I am right in saying that in 1944 or 1945 I had no idea that British Communist Party members and sympathisers, likely to be useful, might be recruited by the Soviet Union as spies. During

137

my brief membership of the party in the early Thirties, when there was talk of 'Moscow gold' in the *Daily Mail* and suchlike despised organs of the capitalist press, Marston used to say he wished a bit of it would filter through to Blackpool, where we scraped along with our local share of members' subs (reduced for the unemployed) and an occasional donation from the town's more affluent left-wingers, like Mr Pablo, ice-cream manufacturer, prosperous, but always reluctant to cough up, since he was said really to favour the Anarchist movement, and he believed any way in self-help, quality displayed in his own business life.

As adumbrated before in these memoirs, one often has the sense that in the course of time ghosts have taken over from the solid, idiosyncratic figures of the past, their milieu ghostly, too; reminders of actuality sometimes strangely occuring, even recurring. When in the Sixties and Seventies I used to go to the Arts Council offices after it had moved from St. James' Square to 105 Piccadilly, passing the end of Berkeley Street could bring back the wartime walk from Rex House to the Ministry of Aircraft Production, housed in a barracklike office block in that null part of Stratton Street parallel with Piccadilly. There, D.N.A.R.'s liaison officer (if I have got his status right) was a plumpish, well-spoken, casually competent young man whom I had previously known, perhaps at *Ariel*, but his name, mutual leg-pulling and technical preoccupations, all have gone. It may be thought that during 1945, in a similarly imperceptible way, war for the chair-borne faded into peace. But even the sedentary had their annals. When the V-1 launching sites were overrun by the Allied advance, that seemed to bring very close Kate and Johnny's move from Blackpool to London. There remained the question of V-2s – the rockets that descended and killed unannounced, and which in a paradoxical way I personally found more disagreeable than the V-1s, whose explosions were preceded by the suspenseful cessation of the sound of their jet engines. Recently, I read that prehistoric man may have lived through eras of terror when Earth was subjected to bombardment by cometary tails: some inkling of that state may have been given by V-2s. It is an indication of our longing to live together again that Kate and Johnny returned before they ceased – foolishly, it now seems, but possibly they were judged to be exhausted, had a deathbed revival.

In 1945, as in the days of Sherlock Holmes, a horse-drawn cab stood for hire at the side of Blackheath Station. When we arrived

(I had met them along the route or perhaps fetched them from Mrs Rosewell's) we hired this vehicle. The luggage was stowed aloft, the horse walked up to the heath and trotted over it to 16 St. John's Park, where the driver did what I had not anticipated – turned without hesitation into the semicircular drive that passed the steps to the front door and led out again into St. John's Park. That this manoeuvre was possible because the drive gates had been permanently propped open on account of a degree of decrepitude did not detract from the grandeur of the gesture. This free access led to a poem called 'Inaction', sometimes anthologised, where a dog enters and urinates on the mudguard of the poet's car, prompting him to think the very animal kingdom is sneering at his cosy life-style. However, the poem was written a fair time later, probably when commitment had ceased even to the Society for Cultural Relations with the U.S.S.R. The arrival by cab was Kate and Johnny's first view of the house, and of the flat we were to live in for no less than a decade.

Perhaps not many V-2s fell after their arrival, but for a brief period we all slept in one room to increase the chance of dying together if hit. One day, in my absence at Rex House, a rocket landed a couple of hundred yards away on the heath, blowing out another window or two, setting the ceiling lights madly swinging, the noise heard by me in the West End (as proved by a subsequent time check). Kate and Johnny walked out to view the smoking crater, touch the warm debris (no doubt like those bombarded peoples of yore), and learn of the escape of a child in a perambulator almost on the spot. It was a bomb story better than any I could produce, but exposure to such risks after bearing years of a renewed sentence in the parental home was a folly explicable only in terms of utter exasperation at waiting for normality.

Because of its modest size, electric fire built into the wall, our mausoleum room was the dining-room, though not affording much protection since above its plasterboard ceiling was mere empty space, topped by the glazed cupola of the billiards-room annexe – pride, no doubt, of some Victorian equivalent of Councillor Marston. It strikes me that the fire featured in one of the few poems I seem to have written at this period, called in fact 'During a Bombardment by V-weapons': the slates mentioned seem to be poetic licence.

The little noises of the house:

Drippings between the slates and ceiling;
From the electric fire's cooling,
Tickings; the dry feet of a mouse.

The poem goes on to claim that these alarm the poet more than the 'ridiculous detonations' produced by the ingenious German rocket-scientists, and that his loved one's pallor poses a worse threat than bombs and bullets:

Now all the permanent and real
Furies are settling in upstairs.

(Again, 'upstairs' was merely notional in the context of reality at 16 St. John's park.) Though improved by her independence at Mrs Rosewell's, Kate had sometimes been far from well during her latter time overlooking Happy Valley. Perhaps one never saw it personally in such journalistic terms, but I suppose many were under strain, under-fed, and generally cheesed-off by the prolonged preposterousness of war. As for the mouse, the Eliotesque image was also rooted in actuality. None of us was blasé about mice. In my grass widowerhood days I often used to eat in the kitchen: as I sat reading in the post-prandial quiet, a mouse might leisurely emerge from between the sliding doors of the under-sink cupboard that concealed pipe-apertures giving only too easy access to the rodent population of the garden and under-floor areas. Though I did not care for these intrusions, I wonder whether I set traps or whether my near-Buddhist prejudice against extinguishing life was already formed. (The poem 'Little Fable' that appeared, with the V-weapons piece, in my *Epitaphs and Occasions* of 1949 was actually written just before the war and featured a mouse of our Blackheath maisonette of that time, when considerations of metre and succinctness probably did not pitch the price of traps very much too low:

The food is covered and a penny trap,
Being bought, is baited with a bacon scrap.)

In the mausoleum room was the HMV portable gramophone acquired in Aberdeen, the historic Menuhin/Elgar fiddle concerto best remembered of the discs played in those days, days perhaps too strange, too uncertain, to be wholly felicitous. The substantial radiogramophone we had spent most of our meagre pre-marriage savings on came out of store U.S., and, as might have been forecast from my Service record in practical matters, I failed to repair it, despite changing a suspect component, the scarce replacement acquired only after much trouble. Some of our possessions were, in fact, like England (and, it could be said, ourselves), rather decrepit.

Even before the German war ended, my former principal at the Woolwich, A. E. Shrimpton, took me to lunch at Scotts by Piccadilly Circus, a venue as impressive as the Hungaria. His war (carrying on the department with meagre forces, serving spare time in the Observer Corps, a wife and three sons to try to keep out of the bombs' way) had been no cake-walk, and he was keen to get me back to the office when peace came; as good a lunch as the wartime West End afforded not without ulterior motive. I should think it was about the same time when Captain Willett told me he had been offered a managing directorship by Marconi's, and wanted to contrive his premature release from the Navy. Whether he judged my literary ability on the draft minutes and so forth I laid before him or, less likely, had heard of, even read, my verse and critical notices, I do not know: however, he asked me for help with the vital letter to their Lordships of the Admiralty. Something quite persuasive must have been concocted, for the letter worked like a charm, and to celebrate the victory the Captain took me to lunch among the red tabs and thick gold braid (right round the sleeve) at the Senior United Services Club on the corner of Waterloo Place opposite the Athenaeum, now, alas, no more. He was succeeded by his deputy, Commander A. S. ('Ben') Bolt, previously rather in his shadow, but on promotion blossoming and doing well. He was youngish, swarthy, polished without being in the least a smoothie, and after the war I saw in *The Times* he had reached flag rank.

Like all organisms, but sooner than most, set-ups in the Services divide, change, and crumble away. Radar training at Lee-on-the-Solent, the special W/T clique at Nairobi, R.N.A.S. Nairobi itself – all examples. One day in Rex House a skirl of bag-pipes was heard echoing along the carpetless corridors, and soon, at the open door of the office I was then in, Commander Crichton appeared, playing the Hibernian instrument, a talent never before suspected. He was in normal naval uniform except that on his head was a bowler hat to which had been affixed a pair of wings, cut out of stiff white paper, presumably symbolic of transference to a different sphere. The Commander was in charge of appointments, had been

141

in fact the man from the Admiralty who had visited *Ariel* at the end of course. He had been 'bowler-hatted', unwillingly retired, no post at Marconi's or anywhere else, and the quite prolonged musical marching was his protest, as out of character as his mastery of wild laments: it brought his displeasure shockingly home, though unfortunately out of earshot of their Lordships. He was based in D.N.A.R. Once when I was alone in his outer office I pulled open a cabinet and had the quickest of squints at my own file. 'An extremely smart officer,' I had time to read, 'who scored 98% in one of his passing-out papers.' The first phrase is authentic: I am reconstructing the second, though the percentage was sensational, the paper being on recent radar equipment of outstanding ingenuity, the answers including descriptions of the journeying of current round the circuits.

Why did I not get on better in life? The glimpse from the outside afforded by Commander Crichton's records raises again the question previously posed in these memoirs, and probably sufficiently answered by the mild adventures described. But such as Lieutenant Hercules demonstrated that great arenas were not essential for effective exercise of the will. When sufficiently goaded (rare event) I was capable of behaving quite as bossily as Hercules: mostly, however, fatally fitted merely to describe him.

I served Captain Bolt as T.A. for quite a spell, but then, in circumstances beyond recall, part of the metamorphotic process referred to, I was moved elsewhere in D.N.A.R. The buzz was that the Department would be set up in Australia the better to conduct its part in the Japanese war, still continuing. Some preliminary shift of the kind may already have taken place: certainly I was under-employed, without a clear role; once more, as in D.A.E., in a room with officers better equipped than I to make work spin out – the room from which I had seen Commander Crichton, enviably sacked. I doubt I was there very long before one day, in August 1945, buying an early *Evening Standard* to read over lunch, I saw a short item in the stop press that seemed to signal a Japanese surrender. Amazing that doubt now exists as to whether it concerned the first or second atomic bomb, fearful events that were to haunt life thereafter, though conviction about the decisiveness of the news item indicates the destruction of Nagasaki. Also, though I write 'to read over lunch', more likely I was as parsimonious about buying evening newspapers as I had been as a law student in London a dozen years before, and only interested in the *Standard* because, warned by Hiroshima, surrender was in the offing. Whether self-interest allowed any feeling for the victims, I wonder.

Relief at the prospect of all hostilities ending was undoubtedly heightened by the virtual escape from the risks of service in the Far East, or at any rate whatever spiritual malaise Australia might have induced. Whether this was happiness, who knows? Before I returned to Rex House I had a few whiskies in Soho, a solitary mini-pub-crawl, for unofficial spirits-rationing compelled one to move on from bar to bar. In my mind's eye I see myself standing in a public bar-room, almost deserted as closing time came up, drink on a scrubbed table (for many Soho pubs still had a village simplicity), gazing out into Dean Street or Frith Street (thorough-fares then quite free of parked cars, dubious emporiums, and vulgar displays), in some kind of historical meditation. Plainly, one longed to be happy. But I had noted as a feature of 'VE Day', the previous May, the absence of the abandon, familiar from photographs and film, of the Armistice of 1918 – in which, indeed, I myself could have participated as a child of six, though whether I should have been moved to behave with excess even on that occasion is unlikely.

How on earth did I occupy my time from the August Japanese surrender to my release from naval service on the 3 December? I see from the scrapbook I was writing a bit during this period for *Tribune* and *Our Time*, as well as *The Listener*, and there is evidence of other literary chores. Rex House may have been the illegal arena for some of this modest activity. Mention of the first two periodicals leads to other recesses of memory, these especially dim. Julian Symons had introduced me as a reviewer to *Tribune* and the left-wing literary magazine *Our Time*. I used occasionally to go into the *Tribune* office in the Strand, where I saw the Literary Editor, Tosco Fyvel, and (though this may have been slightly later) his assistant, the youthful Bruce Bain (who eventually turned entirely into his dramatic critic *nom-de-plume*, Richard Findlater). Tosco must be numbered among the generous and patient editors who encouraged me. I never encountered the famous politicos behind *Tribune* in those days. The *Our Time* office, more squalid, was not far away, in Southampton Street. The editor was Edgell Rickword, poetic hero of my youth and ever after. His assistant, the poet Arnold Rattenbury, youthful as Bruce Bain, fairly soon drifted out of my life, reappearing suddenly so much later that momentarily I scarcely knew who he was. Alas, Edgell died in 1982, at a great age, but Arnold, as devout a Rickword fan as I, is still in touch.

Surely my emotion on encountering Edgell must have exceeded that on lunching in Percy Street with E. M. Forster, though my pre-meeting image is now subsumed in the later actuality – the ragged, drooping moustache, the spectacles with one opaque lens (masking the loss of an eye in the 1914–18 War), the almost inaudible voice, an absence of small talk, comparable with the spectacular deficiencies of Attlee and Arthur Waley, not precluding a sudden succinct and acute literary judgement. The Southampton Street premises had no attractions of their own, but their association in my memory with a general movement towards a pub would have arisen in any case from Edgell's own inclination. I never knew him the worse for drink, but the saloon bar was very much his habitat, perhaps stemming, like his earliest verse, from the pub poets of the Nineties.

Other chambers of recollection might be opened but their furnishings and occupants would prove equally elusive. Schmidt's restaurant and shop in Charlotte Street (writing 'Percy Street' reminds me) was the scene of Saturday lunches with Kathleen and Julian when I was a grass widower, and later; noted for ample helpings of a roughish nature. The vinegary smell of sauerkraut hung ever in the air, and boiled belly of pork was always on the menu: sometimes I ordered the latter with a disregard for dyspepsia amazing to me today. It was there I first met the poet and polymath Jack Lindsay. He was in battledress but I think then working for the Army Bureau of Current Affairs; impressing me sufficiently to put him in my crime novel of a few years later, *Fantasy and Fugue*. With him, as with Arnold, there was a lapse and renewal of acquaintance: he became a neighbour of Bernard Miles and, like me, was enlisted to help with the Sunday evening seasons of 'Poetry at the Mermaid' long, long after the war – an enterprise whose curious connection with Chatham Barracks, a locale of my Ordinary Seaman days, I described in *Vamp*.

These fiction-like *tempi* and links raise considerations not only about the autobiographical art but also about its subject. Reading a biography, though carried along by the sequence of incident, one may pause to wonder what the plot is or is to be. The reflection must be followed immediately by the conclusion – more or less obvious or banal – that the plot of every such volume is the progress towards death. What a phenomenally prolonged preparation for the final few pages, the most compelling and moving! By comparison, an autobiography is plotless: in fact, usually resembles the experi-

144

mental novel (mentioned in *Souvenirs*) I conceived as an adolescent but fortunately made little progress with, a novel beginning normally but gradually getting more and more boring – for childhood has the plot of growing-up as well as incidental freshness and sharpness, whereas (to bring in another art) adulthood is usually mere, and more weakly orchestrated, recapitulation. However, the war, preceded by the threat of war, seems to me to have donated a further plot to the 'growing-up' plot of my life, and the *dénouement* of that further plot – the coming of peace – is, of course, containable in autobiographical form, unlike death.

Autobiography, it may be added, is not the story told about oneself in one's own thoughts. That, for all its distortion and partiality, would involve a detail, a frankness, a truth, a *naiveté* – indeed, a talent – hard to conceive possible. The naturalistic successes and failed artificialities of *Ulysses* indicate the parameters of the problem, and that was fictive.

One's place in the demobilization queue was determined by certain rules. Some temporary officers, however, were in no hurry to go: with two stripes one needed to have quite a decent job to return to in Civvy Street to equal one's pay and allowances. I myself failed to get the Woolwich to come up to scratch. All the same, I was eager to get out of uniform, and with some in the queue willing to be bypassed, and by chatting up the office formerly controlled by Commander Crichton, I was able to some extent to beat the rules. With demobilization leave added on, my service just extended into 1946: almost a lustre.

Even for those who never had the experience, the business of getting a 'demob outfit' at Olympia will have been made familiar by the marvellous little scene at the end of Anthony Powell's *The Military Philosophers*. There in the vast arena, on open stalls that one wandered through and chose from, were all the items of clothing necessary to turn servicemen back to civilians. The assumption was that over the years of war civilian clothes had succumbed to moth or theft or enemy action – or that one had grown out of them through middle-aged spread or muscular development or figgy duff – or even that captivity or dysentery or malaria had caused one to shrink within them. The clothing on display and the mixture of service personnel strolling about gave the sense that already one's uniform was meaningless – the gold stripes on the sleeves, whose acquisition and semi-circularity had caused such concern, of no account, drawing no salutation. In the background, music played

145

but, unlike the ubiquitous barracks Tannoy, muted, sweet, never to be interrupted by a summons to the R.P.O.'s office or the like. In *The Military Philosophers* the narrator encounters, with timeous effect, a figure from his pre-war youth. It comes to me that I myself went along the stalls with someone I knew, accidentally encountered – perhaps the plump young officer from M.A.P., I cannot be sure.

If uniform was suddenly of the past, the clothing acquired was, of course, very much an accompaniment of the future, in the case of some garments a future quite prolonged. I speak in terms of life, not fashion. A painstaking search had to be made for items one could imagine vanity allowing one to wear. I took away the best of the trilby hats simply through thrift, but was never seen out in it – dark blue-grey, with a hard pre-determined shape that included the indentation of the crown. Nick Jenkins in *The Military Philosophers* rejected the underclothes, understandable in a possible patron of Jermyn Street, but for the true skinflint they were acceptable. The shoes reposed in tangled heaps, as in a sale, but I dug into them with determination and came out with a brown pair made by James White & Co., in style not bad, in terms of wear proving simply phenomenal. The riding-mackintosh (was it so dubbed by one of the acolytes at Olympia or did I confer the name ironically thereafter?) was also longevous. Its material was as substantial as that remembered from distant days, stuff turned out by the Windsor Mill, where my father had made his career in rubber-proofing, cut short by untimely death. And it strikes me now for the first time that the material may indeed have been proofed there, the factory continuing its tradition, for its fortune had been founded in Government contracts during the First War. The mackintosh had a single vent at the back, to drape conveniently either side of one's mount, but whether the hacking-jacket I selected had one or two (bugger's delight or bugger's puzzle, as the styles were vulgarly known) I cannot recall, though I liked the greenish garment and wore it through countless weekends. The grey 'slacks' (name still matching the cut) were inferior; not flannel but a material difficult to wear out – though with perseverance I was at last able justifiably to cast them aside, like a long, boring book one is determined to get through.

In *The Military Philosophers*, Jenkins notes the many grey chalk-stripe suits on offer (an alternative to the tweed coat and slacks). The grey was pallid, its sickliness added to by the paler stripe. For a few years it was the uniform of a ghostly army, as it were; its scattered members sitting at office desks, serving in shops, calling for the laundry.

11.   Aftermath

What life to lead and where to go
After the War, after the War?

– Robert Graves

I have presented the answer to the Gravesian question (posed about 'an older bungle') as, in my case, more or less cut and dried; confirmed by prompt action. But I expect I cherished, as before the war, the hope that one day I might do a Trollope – give up my regular profession when I had established sufficient literary fortune. That condition precedent was never fulfilled.

Writing 'Aftermath' at the head of this chapter, the title of Harold Owen's remarkable addendum to his autobiography, makes me more conscious than ever of the unarduous life that followed what could not be described as an arduous war. Though I addressed envelopes for Alderman Reeves, the local Labour candidate in the 1945 General Election, I never contemplated returning to the political activity of the early Thirties. The simple chore, the ambience of the working-class off duty, the gathering of old stalwarts, brought back the previous General Election (of 1935!) referred to in *Vamp*: the intimation was of an anterior incarnation. Ideological questions presented no agonies of choice or renunciation: I believed in live and let live, depressed by the monstrous growth of foolish nationalism, astonishing after the defeat of the fascist powers. If my human equipment was tested it was mainly in the area of health, but none of my complaints precluded a fair amount of nervous and physical energy. Perhaps, indeed, my wonky physical side had some roots in my longing that 'all manner of things shall be well', too cosy an attitude at any historical epoch I have lived through.

A reviewer in the *TLS* (Peter Sedgwick) recently came out with a clever summation that made me grin – the objections of Marcuse and others to the 'deplorable loss of subversiveness once the lustful libido is downgraded in favour of that more reasonable moderator, the ego'. The revolutionaries were actually contemplating a change of emphasis in Freudian theory, but one could substitute the factor of increasing age. Moreover, at seventy one is inclined to job backwards, though as already hinted, after the war one may have been bolshie in the old way for a longer period than now seems plausible. For example, I doubt I would have unquestionably accepted in those post-war days such a notion as Mr Sedgwick characterizes in the same review – Freud's theory 'that human aggression is a drive in its own right, not merely a reaction to the frustration of libido'. I must have gone on believing for some time in human goodness; goodness frustrated only by a society that denied adequate love and power to its most numerous class.

Bob Park, companion of the iffy hut, was one who changed his life after the war, returning to Kenya to work and live despite having displayed absolutely no enthusiasm for the country as a serviceman. I have never seen or communicated with him since our Steptoe and Son life, though can clearly summon up his face and speech as they were forty years ago. Willie Robertson's metamorphosis was perhaps even more surprising: he returned to his Glasgow shipping company, but eventually, starting with the purchase of the building in which his own apartment was situate, profited by the post-war property boom, and became simply a 'property-owner'. He told me about this when we met in the late Forties by appointment 'under the clock' in Charing Cross Station, the first time since Nairobi days. By ill luck it was the moment when x-rays had first confirmed a duodenal ulcer, and I was devoutly obeying a medical injunction not to drink.

We adjourned to a pub in Craven Street where, though disconcerted by my temperance, Willie ordered a Scotch and a beer chaser, perhaps planned in advance, anticipating a serious if brief session (for the whole evening was not free, he or I with some other engagement). The reunion was thus blighted from the outset, though ease and affection were not precluded. But, as is common in such circumstances, neither of us (he less than I) could quite come to terms with the fact that even during the war a great deal had happened to us after we had parted company, symbolized by his having part of a finger missing, the result of a war-time accident. He was, of course, by then habituated to this, but I could not help imagining his original concern, an infinitely worse case than that of the Sunburned Thighs. Characters, too, I but dimly recalled had evidentally subsequently assumed importance in his life: my uninterest in them must have seemed odd.

We never met again. Only through coincidence did I hear of his premature death in the Sixties from a heart attack. An employee of the Woolwich's Glasgow office, Etta Johnstone, knew the family, and naturally Willie and she mutually knowing me had been established. I saw Miss Johnstone regularly at the annual dinners given by the Woolwich for staff members with twenty-five and more years service. The news of Willie was somehow all the sadder for my being aware we should almost certainly never have met again. When *Vamp* was published I sent a copy to Willie's daughter, her address supplied by Miss Johnstone, and subsequently she lent me her father's African and other Navy photographs, some with accompanying 'keys' of names – less familiar, after more than half a lifetime, than the vivid faces. Occasionally, instead of names, the men in the photographs are identified by their towns of origin, a fairly universal Services preoccupation – harmless form of nationalism – and one Willie very much went along with. He was a Paisley man himself; had worked in the centre of Glasgow: was always ready to discuss matters of moment to the local patriot, like the city's tramway system. His death had a grave effect on his wife, bringing poignantly back that ancient concern for her when he was drafted abroad at Lee-on-the-Solent.

Captain Willett passed out of my life on his translation to Marconi's. He died in 1966. Some time after the latter date, the opportunity of dining with his son was thwarted because of illness or some such chance. The opportunity arose not at all because of my former connection with the father, but through an invitation from a mutual friend of mine and the son's. By fictional standards the coincidence would have been accounted strange, for our worlds were far apart. Commander William Willett was regular R.N., like his father, and at the time Private Secretary to the Duke of Edinburgh. Alas, his death was even more untimely than Willie's, and we never met – myself to stay for ever ignorant of the more intimate side of 'Master Basil', and whether he was happy with Marconi's.

Another post-war non-meeting or, strictly, non-reunion, was between Alan Ross and an old destroyer shipmate of lower-deck days, Butcher. Here, I was the mutual friend, for Butcher had worked for the Woolwich before the war, and returned thereafter. He was at branch offices in urban Essex, so I myself saw him only rarely. Whenever I came across him he was sure to say: 'How's old Alan?' – using the adjective *à la* Captain Willett. In later years, when Alan had taken over editorship of the *London Magazine* from John Lehmann and acquired an office, Butch would add: 'One day I'm going to call on old Alan', and get from me confirmation of the magazine's address. In earlier post-war times Butch was perhaps not in the best of odours with the Woolwich, apt at our business conferences to get on his feet too promptly, and speak agin the government. Rebelliousness may also have been expressed on less formal occasions. Whenever I told Alan I had seen Butch, passing on his regards and threat of calling, Alan would recall some incident of their service together, perhaps Butch coming down into the mess off watch from Arctic weather; diminutive, somewhat rotund figure enveloped in a dufflecoat, *New Statesman* protruding from pocket, voluble in barrack-room lawyer style about a grievance or injustice. When Butch retired from the Woolwich he had even more time to call at 30 Thurloe Place, S.W.7., but he never did. The last time I saw him, at one of the dinners for long-serving staff already mentioned, he was looking far from well, had had heart trouble. Not long after that he died. One misses him, no doubt about it.

A poem Alan wrote for my seventieth birthday contains the phrase: 'You bequeathed me/A uniform'. This surely must have been the better of the two, not the somewhat wide-in-the-hips serge. Younger than I, and unmarried, Alan's Order of Release came after mine; in fact, he was kept on for a while to interpret, and do intelligence work, in occupied Germany, possibly with Sub-Lieutenant the Lord Holden, so required another uniform. Taller than I, he would have needed to lengthen his braces. Later still, there was a further bequest, of my greatcoat, which I had worn for a bit in Civvy Street, having had the epaulettes removed and the brass buttons changed for ordinary black ones, useful when he came to watch Charlton Athletic, standing with us on the great exposed south slope at the Valley. During this further sartorial history I must have regretted not opting originally for the more disguisable watch coat.

Alan's post-war spiritual uncertainty seemed evident despite his respectable occupations on demobilization – at first with the British Council, then with the *Observer*. In my case, the war's upsets were perhaps indicated by the length of time between *A Lost Season* and my next book of poems, *Epitaphs and Occasions* (1949). By that time I had eased myself into writing fiction for adults by producing, after *Savage Gold*, a crime story for teenagers, *With My Little Eye* (1948), which was actually published in the United States as an adult novel.

After quitting the army, Julian Symons had become an advertising copywriter. He inherited from George Orwell a weekly book page in the *Manchester Evening News*, and in 1947 took up the life of a man of letters. Through unremitting industry, jealously noted before in these memoirs, he succeeded; greatly to his credit retaining the critical standards of the old days and never entirely giving up poetry. After a few years he and Kathleen moved into the country from the top flat in 16 St. John's Park (and continued to oscillate between Kent and South London), but we stayed close friends, and with Kathleen's brother, Jack Clark. In 1945 the myriad events and changes of middle years lay enigmatically ahead, less complex in one's own hacking-jacketed and riding-mackintoshed case than in that of most of one's friends.

In the summer of 1982, Norman Lees came to visit us, with his wife B. When I first knew him, myself only seventeen, if that, he was the engrossing clerk with the Blackpool solicitors I was articled to. Subsequently he gained his articles, qualified, practised on his own and in partnership, and was now virtually retired, a consultant to his firm. While I was in Africa weekly visits to Norman and B had helped sustain Kate's morale, but since the war meetings had necessarily been few and far between. Their having read *Souvenirs* stimulated talk of bygone days, not that stimulation was required. I will ration myself to one chain of connections that emerged – connections that possibly these memoirs have become too obsessive about, copying old age itself. An acquaintance of Lees, older, in his late seventies, fellow member of the golf-club I might have joined as a young solicitor to demonstrate my client-acquiring faculty, expressed a wish to read *Souvenirs*, having heard of it through the local newspaper or perhaps Lees's conversation, though never on his own initiative having read a book in his life. He borrowed Lees's copy; said, when he returned it, that he had enjoyed it, found it interesting, and as a boy had often played with Willie Vero.

At risk of tedium, I will briefly recount something of what was

151

said in *Souvenirs* about this last-mentioned character, named like a Nineties poet. With Kate and me the name is a synonym for Rachmaninov's Prelude in C sharp minor, though it comes from a period of my life long before I met her. He was the son of the widow or *femme-sole* in whose house my mother and brother and I were lodgers after my father's death in 1920. Little more than his raven hair, eagle nose, lean figure, penchant for doing dialogues in assumed voices, and repeatedly playing the then not quite so notorious Prelude, seemed to remain until Lees's acquaintance gave the legend historical confirmation. Mr Peele used to take the Vero house for summer holidays from Oldham (ourselves taking next door), and it may well have been there that his elder daughter introduced me to cream-cracker sandwiches. And I insert here an observation that has been in my mind ever since I first read *Remembrance of Things Past*. When we travelled to Blackpool from Oldham by train, we were always on the *qui vive* for the first glimpse of the Tower (and by its side in those days, the Big Wheel), coming into view from quite a distance over the Fylde plain, and appearing now through the windows of one side of the compartment, now the other, like the steeples of Martinville. As those twin spires to Marcel, so the far sight of the vulgar artifacts of Blackpool gave to me an 'obscure sense of pleasure' – at least they did before my father's premature death led us to live in permanent propinquity to them, both in and out of holiday time.

It so happens that among the score or two of scribbled notes remaining of matters for possible mention in these memoirs is one relating to a summer holiday at the house next to Mrs Vero's. In bed, in a room alone, I woke to the light of day. Hearing voices below, I thought I had overslept, and hurriedly dressed, even though I had never before in my life dressed entirely 'without supervision' (as I used to say, years later, applying for assistant solicitors' jobs). But when I went downstairs I found it was still evening, not morning, the period being one when, like Marcel, 'I used to go to bed early.'

How characteristic the rapid, nervous attempt to right a situation that had elements of the adverse or blameworthy! Almost equally so the recognition of the underlying naive folly that would detract, even in my puerile mind of that ancient day, from the praise for achieving a fully-clothed state. Moreover, I would be profoundly embarrassed at even momentarily displaying a comic persona, as though qualifying for that genus of such so often smiled at in these

152

pages. I see that several of the scribbled notes reveal me not dissimilarly, incidents from widely separated stages of my life that I refrain from delineating not so much because they can't easily be worked in as for fear of labouring their ironic connotation. Besides, even towards the end of so supreme an egotistical exercise as this, one fears mere accumulation of the personal.

This is the place to mention, if at all, another category of note, a typical example being: 'Have I written about trouser-presses?' At school, possession of such a machine denoted rather more than mere chic, something hard to put a name to; neither know-how, quite, nor family affluence. The device must now be practically unknown, possibly sold at a ludicrous price as a 'bygone', even an 'antique', from market stalls. Trousers were put between two sets of hardwood boards and large butterfly-screws tightened on four bolts, so to impart a crease if left overnight. I say butterfly-screws, but I was chagrined to find, after prevailing on my mother to buy me a press, a contemporary, the otherwise despised A. P. Ames (Gorill, as nicknamed), brought to school at the start of the same term a press with screws (technical name not known) whose wings did not descend the bolt but remained conveniently in the palm of the hand, like a tap.

I well recall inserting the trousers of my first suit of 'longs' in my press – 'long' trousers a category turned historical in my lifetime, for shorts are not now worn away from sports arenas, even male infants wearing pants concertinaed down to the shoes, like shabby midgets. To my amazement, my friend S. H. Birch (never before heard from, or seen, since our schooldays) said during the correspondence prompted by *Souvenirs* that he remembered the suit – raiment that gave me, like much in life ostensibly trivial, such heartache on account of its deficiencies. Also vivid is the way a small portion of trousers could easily involve itself with a bolt and screw, and the creases be thus impresssed with undesired squiggles – a result due rather less to carelessness than to the somewhat cheeseparing size of the press, a further deficiency compared with Gorill's.

In one of the couple of letters written to me in 1968 by Jack Jolly, the balladeering R.A.F. Sergeant, he said he was five years my junior and had worked in H.M. Customs since the war. So now he will have achieved retirement, or be sweating on the top line therefor. Hard to believe that at Tanga he was only twenty-four or -five, little more than my eldest grand-daughter now. I had asked him, replying to his initial letter, what 'he had done with his life'.

153

In the light of my supposed fame his answer was excessively modest. I might have responded that even an Oxford Professor of Poetry has only one life, and fails, like most, to do the best with it.

Just before writing these final paragraphs I went into the roofspace and looked into a suitcase unopened for years. The action was occasioned by my son wondering if I had some early archives of his. Those were not unearthed, but by accident I did discover the 'ring-file of typescripts', poems from the Thirties and a few items from 1940, which (*Vamp* recounts the business) I had come to think was a figment of imagination – the output of the period in mind being rather in a Memoranda or Minute Book brought to light previously. The ring-file also included MS poems, and with it were two notebooks containing work of the period, mostly verse. No treasure-trove must be envisaged: the overall impression given is of scruffiness and mediocrity. But the discovery brings home once more the multiplicity of the actual compared with the filleted effect of memory. Some of the pieces thrown up had appeared in my 1939 volume *Poems*, others in periodicals of the day. I may say that one item is a draft of the penis or sexy lighthouse poem, but it does not help with the vexed adjectival question (Anthony Powell, after reading *Vamp*, where the matter is ventilated, suggested 'phallic' as a solution). Apparently, I was slightly more industrious at St. Mary's Bay than *Vamp* allowed, for there is also a draft piece of greater length, unpublished and forgotten, to set against the enviable output of the two other poets on that curious 1938 holiday, Julian Symons and H. B. Mallalieu.

A further MS poem of 1938 seems apposite enough to reproduce. Though its *genre* is the dramatic monologue, blending the ancient and modern worlds in a mode I was to exploit after the war in such poems as *The Ides of March* and *On the Mountain*, some of the sentiments expressed must have come from the heart of R. B. Fuller (as I still used to sign my verse):

> I have no interest in my childhood,
> I might as well not have lived it.
> Nor am I concerned about the infancy of others,
> No one need write of it or speak of it for me.
> I am not much bothered with my life now,
> My life tomorrow, in twenty years,
> And not at all with the other life of others.
> I speak to myself seldom of my character,

Rather more often I regard my face,
And say to the glass 'Here is that one who
Perceives reality with a particular body.'
I do not look others in the eye, I cannot
Distinguish the villain or the liar.
I am equally trusting and untrusting
And specially amiable to those I fear.

I live with several ideas
Like a man with large and unfriendly dogs.
One is the end of the world in my time
Which I mention in my almanacks.
My life I see lost in a loud year in history,
My dates linked with a curving line and captionned,
And childhood, youth and this stuck on a skewer.

As these memoirs prove, I did in the end get round to my childhood; and I feel the war made me, at least for the time being, less narcissistic. It did not bracket my dates, for which I have been duly thankful, though it left me with the idea of 'the end of the world in my time' vastly sharper and more hurtful.

But I cannot end quite here. Checking in the London Library my memory of the name of Charles Peace's Blackheath victim, I took down the relevant volume in the 'Notable British Trials' series, saw Peace's misdoings rather more complex and interesting than imagined, and brought the book home. With nice obliquity, it begins with the trial of the Habron brothers for a murder to which Peace later confessed, thus securing a free pardon for the convicted brother, whose death sentence had fortunately been commuted to life imprisonment. The murder took place in Whalley Range, a Manchester suburb whose respectability is emphasised, and which readers of *Souvenirs* may remember as the home of the 'rotten beggar Byng', tormentor of Gorill at Seafolde House. The Habrons worked in a market garden, the 'slutchy' condition of which came into the matter – an epithet I have probably not myself used since before Gorill days. A couple of witnesses referred to a man wearing a 'pot-hat'. Seeing this noun, one momentarily wondered if a printer's error had not reversed the first syllable; then, with an almost Proustian flood of association, its meaning – a synonym for 'bowler-hat' – came back, the word unencountered for sixty years. My grandfather would have referred to that headgear as a pot-hat;

155

wore one himself, certainly in his mayoral year; would have warmed the interior at the fire (with his gloves and the handle of his stick) before venturing into the open air – a performance not lacking elements of exaggerated play-acting and which I must surely have touched on somewhere before. I think he would not have said 'slutchy' except on the occasions when to amuse he adopted a proletarian manner of speech – just as I do not recall him using the similarly expressive 'slur' except in an enigmatic catch-phrase, of origin now unknown to me, 'Blow thee nose and slur whum' ('Blow your nose and slide home').

One of the plates in *Trials of Charles Frederick Peace* is of the rear of 2 St. John's Park. I can see the reality through the window as I write this at my desk, for when at last we moved from 16 St. John's Park we actually went nearer to number 2, to a small house we built in the lane running along the rear gardens of St. John's Park. The *Trials* was published in 1926; the photograph for the plate may have not been taken until just before then. However that may be, the place is virtually unchanged, though until recently a private hotel. We once had a curious relationship with an ancient permanent resident therein, which I will forbear to describe. No wonder one was fictionally bogged down for so long in the turbid stream of consciousness.

Appendix

The Sick Bay

When I went into the sick bay with suspected malaria I was put into a ward of three beds: there was already another petty officer there whom I didn't know and, in the corner, the chief bosun's mate. The P.O. had malaria as well: he was very deep under the bedclothes. The Buffer had merely some skin trouble and I could see that he was his usual ramrodesque, tight-lipped self even in bed. I undressed, put on the supplied pyjamas (torn, typically, in the trousers part); I was a bit shivery but not too bad – on the bedside table I'd put Gilchrist's *Life of Blake* and my notebook and fountain pen, but when I got between the one sheet and one blanket I looked at them and turned over.

I kept coming out of the doze to attend to various incidents. A civilian woman ambulance driver of dangerous age brought me, smiling bewitchingly, an iced drink with pieces of paw-paw in it. I was surprised to find how much I needed it. Someone took my temperature again and roused the P.O. next to me. I glimpsed a craggy face. There was some difficulty in bringing him to deal with the realities of temperature and pulse taking. The Buffer kept having interviews with his minions. Normally he plays on this station what I cannot but regard as a curious role: twice a day he is at the front of the parade, calling it to attention in his powerful voice and reporting it correct to the duty officer, but the rest of his time is spent in looking after some fowls at the top of the camp. 'You can shut up the drakes now,' I heard him telling an A.B. Cups of tea were brought by an African and at last someone came and pricked my finger and smeared a few slides with blood. A sick berth tiffy came to straighten my bed and said 'Where's your other sheet?'

The Buffer ate his dinner sitting stiffly up in bed, munching with iron jaws and staring impassively in front of him. Afterwards he got up and shaved with an open razor, one hand on his hip, lathering himself three times and taking it off with loud scraping noises. I kept sinking into deep dozes. A sick berth tiffy woke me out of one of them and said the blood test showed that I had sub-tertian malaria,

157

and later I took two five-grain tablets of quinine. At five o'clock I thought it was the middle of the night. I kept having difficulty in getting my bearings in the room.

The next morning they carried the other P.O. and me in our beds to another ward which they were turning into a malaria ward. I felt more rational. Quite early an A.B. in overalls had arrived carrying a pot of paint, and under the directions of the Buffer had started picking out some of the timbers of the hut in a cool white. These timbers were round the Buffer's bed. I wondered what it was all for, but I was moved before I found out.

In the new ward there were six beds, four of them occupied. In the other two occupied beds were young men whose temperatures were now normal: they carried on back chat with the sick berth tiffies and demanded food and were generally tiresome. A sick berth tiffy came to straighten my bed in readiness for the medical officer's rounds and said 'Where's your other sheet?' And then the leading tiffy appeared at the door and said 'Attention in the ward. Books and papers away,' and the quack came in. The P.O., who was in the next bed to me, was brought out of his underworld of bedclothes. The quack said 'Have you any pains?' The P.O. didn't move a muscle. 'Have you a headache? Any pains?' After a pause the P.O. said, certainly not in reply, 'I've got a headache.' The quack looked a bit startled, and went on.

The next morning the P.O. rose out of the bedclothes like the Kraken and everyone got a good view of him for the first time. He was better. He had soft hair, the colour of apricot jam, the kind that imperceptibly turns grey, scattered thinly over his head: his face was amiable and shapeless, his skin like a shark's. The back of his head had that peculiar flatness that goes with a neck cracked like a dried mud bed. Old blurred tattooing covered his arms and chest. After breakfast another P.O. of similar age came to see him, and then it was apparent what sort of a man he was, what sort of a life he led. These are puzzling questions to me when I put them in relation to certain people. Normally I am not sufficiently interested to put them at all: but when one is sick I think one's mind tends to work like that of a novelist. I am always fascinated by those novels which deal with complicated relationships between complicated people; I admire them but am puzzled because it seems to me that people, including myself, are extremely simple and so are their relationships. The people in Jonson and Dickens are for me done quite adequately: they are all humours or caricatures but so I find most people in real life. How can one understand the Buffer except by regarding him simply as a curiosity, a phenomenon no thicker than a piece of paper: a man who spends his life calling parades to attention, keeping fowls and having things painted white?

So with the P.O. His mate came to tell him of what had happened in their world.

'There was a warrant read this morning,' said the mate. 'Old Budgie dipped a badge.' (That is to say, lost a good conduct stripe.)

'Dipped a badge?' echoed the P.O. 'Old Budgie dipped a b . . .' And here we heard for the first time what was to become very familiar – the P.O.'s characteristic laugh. The last few words went into an asthmatic falsetto of increasing painfulness and unintelligibility (the knobbly face turning bright pink, the lips retracting to reveal a mass of gold and ivory) until at last, to one's relief, it broke into a raucous guffaw. The mate laughed as well and then said:

'We had a night last night.'

'Mm?' said the P.O.

'Mingi beer. There was mingi bottles in the Empire bar.'

'Mingi beer, eh?' said the P.O.

'I woke up this morning on the floor with Jan – as usual,' said the mate. They both laughed again.

This was it; this was the P.O.'s life – the creation from day to day of a legend surrounding himself and his friends. Half the time he is telling it, like Homer: the other half, like Ulysses, making it. The details of Budgie's affair and of the booze-up at the Empire will pass into the legend and take their place beside the terrible fight with the cops in New York, the wrecking of the bag-shanty in Mombasa, and the other tales that tumble out of his mouth like a jack-pot.

All this time a dreadful nausea from the quinine was growing in me, and at length I began to vomit after the doses. The tear in the trousers part of the pyjamas kept lengthening and became an irritation. I regarded everything with disfavour, including the two other people in the ward, particularly a boy of nineteen called Leonard. He was a cook; a thin lad with a pale peaky face and a perpetual look of surprise, eyebrows slightly raised, mouth slightly open. Whatever he had to say he said with this expression, letting his words reedily out with the greatest air of indifference, as though he barely expected to be heard or understood. And certainly, at first, he was barely understood by me; he had a Northumberland accent of a breadth I had never come across before. Next to the Brums I think the Geordies are the worst speaking bastards in England, but Leonard I put into the Brum class. His vowels were quite foreign. For no he said 'nee'; for do, 'dee'. Mouth was 'mooth'; night was 'neet'. I wish I could adequately write the indescribable distortion he made of the vowel sound in walk – 'wawrlk', he said, or something. I lay, massaging ineffectively my hedgehog-housing stomach, and listened to him, trying to translate as he went execrably along. I felt viciously towards him.

The other boy was Welsh with long blonde hair brushed straight back and a constant smile. A dance tune on the gramophone set him hissing rhythmically between his teeth. The man who set the gramophone going was another horror, a little, immensely cocky, sick berth tiffy, also Welsh. He came briskly in at lunch-time and said, in his quick voice, 'What about some good music, eh? Nothing like it. Ever heard of Borodin, Leonard?' He put the accent on the second syllable: Leonard continued his surprised look at the world and did not bother to reply. 'He wrote some very good music. This is called Prince Eyegor. Very good it is.' Sure enough we had a side of the Polovtsian Dances which I could not enjoy in the least because of him who had put it on. And then Artie Shaw played and Blondie hissed.

The day wore on. At night someone from the outside world came in the ward to see the young boys, and offered to go to the N.A.A.F.I. for them. Leonard

159

wanted a number of things 'and two bottles of pop to clean me mooth oot.' The P.O. was asked what he wanted. 'Two bottles,' he said. 'Pop?' 'No – beer,' he said and went into an asthmatic convulsion. We were all inside our mosquito nets which draped the beds and went up to the ceiling in narrowing funnels, the lights above each bed lighting them up in a ghostly way. Outside, the night was chill and dark blue with occasional cries of animals. I dozed and was wakened by a great gurgling and the voice of the P.O. gleefully saying. 'Cor, that's good.' He had got the beer. And later again, when the lights had all gone out and only the moon illuminated the room, I heard the surreptitious clanking of a bottle and then a horrible gasping and gulping. Another legend was being created: how even in the middle of malaria, in the prison-house of the sick bay, he'd had his beer. 'You silly old b–', I murmured to myself as I went off to sleep again, 'You silly old b–'.

The next day the quack put me off quinine and on atebrin and ordered me a dose of bismuth to settle my stomach. I became much better and began to read *The Life of Blake*. The P.O. was up in the afternoon and went away for a couple of hours to seek his mate. I was still wearing, intolerably, the tattered pyjama trousers, and when a sick berth tiffy came to make my bed he said 'Where's your second sheet?' The dangerous ambulance driver passed smiling through the ward. There was a discussion in which Leonard maintained that Kilimanjaro was the highest moontin in the world. But the nightmare edge of these sick bay characters had been taken off – for me, at any rate. The Jonsons in their genius retain always the vision given by a high temperature: we others have to go back to a less coloured, a less exciting world of people.

'The eyes of fire,' I read, 'the nostrils of air, the mouth of water, the beard of earth.' And 'The head Sublime, the heart Pathos, the genitals Beauty, the hands and feet Proportion.' It is all very interesting but it has not very much to do with having malaria in the sick bay.

The People Round About

I was sent on my convalescent leave in about an hour, due to the combined efforts of the charitable organisation which arranges such things and the station Regulating Petty Officer. He is not really an R.P.O., but a seaman P.O., called Scouse Marshall, acting as such and very fed up about it. He says that, on the whole, he'd rather be at sea. He filled up with slow and heavy pen my leave ticket and was vague about where I was going and sighed frequently. He said he had gut trouble: it is all the sitting at a desk and writing he has to do as acting R.P.O. which has got him down. He is a very nice bloke, indeed, but he didn't arrange transport for me, and I had to hitch-hike with my suitcase to the offices of the charitable organisation.

From there I was whisked away in a great American automobile a hundred miles to this swagger hotel which looks out at the mountain, first over deep green valleys and then brown game-covered plains. When I was sitting in the bar the first night an Army Captain came and spoke to me, and all the time I have gone about with him, under his influence doing things I never should have done, like playing squash and golf and tennis. He is in his early twenties, good looking, but not tall, and he wants, when the war is over, to buy a sailing boat and sail away. His favourite authors are Sabatini and Jeffery Farnol, and he plays selections from musical comedies on the reverberating hotel piano. I find him very likeable and already I tease him gently about his green silk polka-dotted scarf and his half-hearted search for unattached girls.

The rest of the residents almost all have their points of interest. Some of my friends say I ought to write prose, and this being on my conscience I have been thinking of making up a story about the people in the hotel and round about. Whenever I think of a plot the same idea always comes into my head – a young man meets a beautiful woman and then something tragic or ironic happens to one or both of them. But this will not do at all for these people, as you will see when I describe a few of them. I become more and more uncertain about the relationship between life and prose fiction. I begin to think that I do not see enough complication in the former to be able to write the latter. It is some deficiency in my imagination or observation, or, worse still, in the way I live. For instance (if it is for instance) I am writing this in the bar, and at the next table there is a mild, tall military man with a clipped grey moustache and next to his beer is lying an unopened book which he has borrowed from the hotel library. The book is Kafka's *America*. It is clear to me that he will return the book to the library in amazement after having read a few pages. He has been deluded by the title. That is about the depth I see in the life which goes on around me. It is fairly amusing but not profound.

The most delightful character in the hotel is a man who looks very much like the film actor, Conrad Veidt. He is an army officer but wears plain clothes all the time – such things as corduroy trousers, yellow shirts, sports coats slashed with leather, and on Saturday night, when there was a dance in the hotel, a dinner-jacket with black mosquito boots. I have never seen anyone with such a consistently straight back. Eating, drinking or playing the gambling machine in the bar, his back is vertical, as straight as his nose, and his well-shaped nostrils are from time to time slightly dilated. His hair is brilliantined and brushed straight back. This gambling machine is an old-fashioned one, where you catch steel balls between two parallel movable arms: the balls come down between a mesh of pins, so quickly and irregularly that it is very difficult to take any money out of the machine at all, and it is a shilling a go. Nevertheless, the machine is very popular and forms a topic of conversation and a focal point for people in the bar, whose faces light up as soon as anyone puts a shilling in it. Very often it is Conrad Veidt who is sitting in front of it on a high stool, marvellously erect and masterful, his elbows tucked in, his whisky-and-soda and a pile of shillings on top of the machine. 'It's so *frightfully* wearing,' he says. 'It makes me boss-eyed.' But he goes on playing. His young, dark and decorative wife, who wears trousers and drinks beer, stands by his side.

The nicest man is about forty-five and rather shaky, having been blown up in some part of the war. He totters about ready to be amiable, with a book under his arm, which he reads over his solitary meals. At the bar one night he and the Captain and I played the golf game with the poker dice which are always on the bar counter. When he was throwing for the last of his five knaves, he kept turning out a queen. 'Here's that dreadful woman again!' he cried, his mouth twitching under his moustache. He encourages Conrad Veidt at the gambling machines and sometimes self-deprecatingly plays a game himself. I wonder whether perhaps he is not *rather* complicated.

But I look round at the plump women with small children, at the hook-nosed old woman, svelte in her trousers, who plays fierce table tennis, gripping a long cigarette-holder between her teeth; at the heavy porcine man with the moustache and the monocle; the blond, beautiful, but weak honeymoon couple; and listen to the talk and am reassured. Early morning tea, dressing, breakfast, fishing, pre-lunch drink, golf, tea, squash or tennis, bath, pre-dinner drinks, the machine, dinner, post-dinner drinks, bed – time is not elastic enough to be complicated in.

One day the Captain went up one of the rivers to fish, and I went with him. We drove along the red roads which have been cut in the sides of the valleys until we came to a fishing camp by the side of the fast river. There the Captain walked up and down, flicking the water, and I watched him or read a book. This river is in the native reserve and, of course, all around us the Africans were carrying on their normal life, except the boy the Captain had got to follow him about and carry his fishing satchel. The maize the Africans were growing came down almost to the river's edge. There were paths through it down the sides of the valley where small boys or old men brought sheep and cattle to water and let them crop the indifferent grass which grew on the river bank. The sheep were small with long legs and a reddish-brown colour like the soil: perhaps they were that colour because they were dirty. The cattle were the usual humped, emaciated native cattle, and the small boys thwacked their corrugated ribs with sticks. All day these children looked after the beasts: I wondered if they ever played. At the hotel children with names like Michael and Nicholas play all day, trotting about and giggling endlessly. These African children, I thought sententiously, are already old. The ancient men who came down were tremendously impassive: they had polished sepia skulls and a fringe of curled white hair; they were toothless, and stood with their wrinkled buttocks and their staffs, held by a hand at each end, horizontally behind their necks in the way Africans have. Some of them wore sheepskin cloaks and they were decorated with a few bead ornaments and feathers. They controlled the cattle with contempt and looked at no one. When they went back through the crops it seemed as if they were going away to die. The young, I saw when I had thought about it, were certainly young and the old were fixed at another pole of life. By the wooden bridge there were some girls sitting, laughing and chewing sugar cane: the thing was quite complete. The cloths and rags these people were dressed in were the colour of the earth; of the sheep. It is difficult to compare such values, but the tribe in its pre-history looks as though it is living rather better than we

162

are. Its only history, fortunately, is natural calamities. I do not envy these people. I only note their different responsibilities, the absence of feverishness in their worn-out men, and their precise and placid adaptation to things like starvation, and even death. In contrast to them, I certainly do think about incidents like an old man with a yellow cracked neck at the dance on Saturday night bringing a girl to the bar for a drink and as he did so writhing himself against her bosom and grinning. It was quite a natural thing to do, but I am sure an African would relieve himself of his desires in a more civilized and dignified way.

At lunch-time we had our hard-boiled eggs and beef sandwiches and beer, and the Captain's boy lay a nice distance away with nothing to eat. After that the Captain caught a trout, and both he and the boy were very pleased. We drove back to the hotel in time for tea.

And then a curious and terrible thing happened. Two days later we went out shooting over the plains, and in the middle of the day came to a farm belonging to some people the Captain knew and whose permission to shoot on their land we wanted to get. The plains were between this farm and the mountain, and to get there we had driven over a bad track between the last thorn trees and the beginnings of a more luxurious vegetation, the land getting higher and more broken. At last we came out at a wooden house which had an enclosed, parched lawn in front of it, and on the lawn a dog as big as a native cow, which came and banged itself up against us, making me nervous until I saw that it was not dangerous but foolish. The woman of the house came out and the Captain introduced me: she was called Mrs Rickman and was in her forties, very pleasant, with grey hair and an alert face. We went into the house and sat on chintz-covered arm-chairs in a large room, and I noticed the cheap old-fashioned reproductions on the walls and the scriptural commentaries on the bookshelves and the, nevertheless, air of luxury and comfort. The Captain and Mrs Rickman were asking each other about mutual acquaintances, and she told us of her nephew, who was a bomber pilot really, but who had just, after months of effort and agitation, achieved his dearest ambition and got in a fighter squadron.

'What are *you* in now, David?' she asked.

'Ordnance,' said the Captain.

'How *dull!*'

Indeed, it was dull after her stories of harassed town majors in Abyssinia and the frightfully important missions to Australia, and I felt sorry for the Captain, who was murmuring something and going rather pink.

'How big is your place here?' I asked Mrs Rickman, to cover him up. Her intelligent eyes were puzzled.

'I mean,' I went on, 'how many acres do you farm?'

Her look at me made the question seem slightly stupid – or impertinent – though I couldn't understand the reason for the look.

'Oh, about twenty thousand,' she said, and went immediately on to another subject. She was almost a brilliant talker. She had left England in 1920; a *flapper* then, she still salted her talk with what I suppose must have been the slang of

1920. *Ripping*, she used as an adjective more than once; it was quite charming. David asked her about the fishing up in the hills. It was less good, she said. 'The boys, *all* of them, are fishing now. Isn't it *disgusting?*' She meant that the Africans who lived up the river were fishing it. I happily stored this remark up to produce later as evidence of the state of the colonial mind.

And then we brought in our mutton sandwiches and hard-boiled eggs and beer, and she had a boy bring in some more picnicky food, and we all had lunch still sitting in our arm-chairs. The dog came in and lumbered about for scraps, knocking glasses over and treading on the plates. We could hardly see each other when he was in the middle of us. Mrs Rickman started telling us about three fellows from the Fleet Air Arm who had been spending their leave on the next farm. They had been out shooting and when they had got back one of them had pulled a shotgun, muzzle first, out of the back of the car. The gun was loaded and in some remarkable manner had gone off. The bulk of the charge had blown the ball of the man's thumb off; a few scattered pellets had gone in his head and neck. Mrs Rickman was sent for because she'd had nursing experience, and she'd treated him for shock before he was taken, in the car, to hospital. The loss of blood from the thumb was the worst thing, she said; there was a pellet in the gum, one in the frontal sinus, one in the cheek, and another in the neck; but they had not penetrated very deeply, and it was all more unfortunate than dangerous.

'I think it was number four shot,' said Mrs Rickman. 'Isn't that *rather* big?'

'Yes, it is,' said the Captain, and then he said: 'Fuller is in the Fleet Air Arm.'

'Oh, *are* you?' said Mrs Rickman. 'Then perhaps you know this poor fellow.'

'Do you remember his name?' I asked her.

She did. It was Petty Officer Marshall.

'I know him,' I said, 'quite well.'

'*Really!*' I think they both said.

As we left, David asked: 'May we shoot a tommy?'

'Yes, *do*,' said Mrs Rickman. 'And if you go down by the river there are scores of pig. You can shoot them all – they're *such* a nuisance.'

We went by the river and the Captain also shot at several tommies, which are a kind of small gazelle, but quite without result. He was even more disgusted with this performance than with his one trout in one day.

The next day, while we were having a drink at the other and less good hotel in this place, I met a man I knew called Black, who was there on a holiday. I really cannot be bothered to describe Black, he is such a null sort of person. When we had expressed mutual surprise and chatted a little, he said: 'Was that petty officer who had a shooting accident here a friend of yours?'

'I know him,' I said.

'Did you know he was dead?'

The pellet in the neck had caused an haemorrhage and he'd been asphyxiated, so Black said. No one at the hospital had thought the thing very serious. Black was friendly with the local padre (he would be), who had also a commission in the army and was the chaplain attached to the hospital, and this was the way Black knew about it.

Black and the Captain started talking about the shooting and fishing. The Captain said that the car he had been hiring was suddenly unavailable, and asked Black how he got about. Black borrowed the padre's car. 'I'm leaving tomorrow,' he said. 'Why don't you try to get hold of it? Mention my name.' In the end we went to see the padre. He was a tall, gaunt man with a freckled skin, dressed in a khaki cardigan and shorts, with a pipe between his great teeth. He most amiably refused us the loan of his car, and then, to make amends, told us about the local fishing, with a wealth of detail which to me was extremely boring. It was like a sermon; he made the rivers the main headings, their best stretches the interminable sub-headings. His voice was slow and precise, his sentences too well constructed. In my new rôle of prose writer I tried to remember some of the technical things. 'What fly have you used?' he asked the Captain penetratingly. The Captain was evasive; as a matter of fact he had used almost all the flies in his tin, including some very picturesque ones he didn't even know the name of. 'Use a Coachman,' said the padre, as though he were giving him the formula for the good life. 'Unless the water has been thrashed, use a Coachman.' And then the padre turned to me: he had observed my cap badge, my white shorts and blue jersey.

'Did you know,' he said in the same voice, 'this petty officer I'm burying today?' And then we got away. 'Tight lines to you,' he said as we went.

The weather has been very cloudy and the mountain only visible once. This was one evening when the obscured sun shone on the snow which streaks, high up in the sky, the jagged peak. A *frisson* of something went through me as I looked at it for a minute and then went to join the Captain at the bar and to talk about and try to guess the relationships and occupations of the intriguing new arrivals. Often, when I am alone, I think of Scouse Marshall, dead, and the way he died and how I got to know about it. Such things seem hardly to be connected with life as it normally goes on with these people round about me, or even with the Africans. It is as though in the lounge the heavy-moustached, monocled man, instead of asking me politely (as he did a moment ago) for the *Tatler*, on which I was resting my paper, had said sadly, as he bent over me: 'I have an incurable cancer.'